Letters in
American History

LETTERS IN AMERICAN HISTORY

WORDS TO REMEMBER
1770 TO THE PRESENT

EDITED BY
H. JACK LANG

HARMONY BOOKS/NEW YORK

Every effort has been made to trace the copyright holders of the letters used in this book. Should there be any omission in this respect we apologize, and shall be pleased to make the appropriate acknowledgment in any future printings.

Grateful acknowledgment is hereby made to the following publishers and individuals for permission to reprint the material specified:

Letter from Hashime Saito to Abigail Van Buren. Copyright, 1980, Universal Press Syndicate. Reprinted with permission. All rights reserved. (Taken from the Dear Abby column.)

Letter from Anne Morrow Lindbergh to her husband, July 2, 1944, from *War Within and Without: Diaries and Letters of Anne Morrow Lindbergh*, copyright © 1980 by Anne Morrow Lindbergh. Reprinted by permission of Harcourt Brace Jovanovich, Inc.

Letter from Captain Robert Peterson, reprinted with permission from the May 1951 *Reader's Digest*.

Letter from Lee H. Oswald to John B. Connally, Jr., *Four Days: The Historical Record of the Death of President Kennedy*, compiled by United Press International and American Heritage Press © 1964 by American Heritage Publishing Co., Inc. and United Press International.

Letter from Codman Hislop to Noah Webster, Jr., Esquire, Union College Symposium, vol. 1, no. 1, Winter 1962.

Letter from Bill Lederer to Admiral McDonald from *The Saturday Evening Post* © 1962 The Curtis Publishing Company.

Designed by Wendy Cohen

Copyright © 1982 by H. Jack Lang

Published by Harmony Books, a division of Crown Publishers, Inc., One Park Avenue, New York, New York 10016, and simultaneously in Canada by General Publishing Company Limited

HARMONY BOOKS and colophon are trademarks of Crown Publishers, Inc.

Manufactured in the United States of America

Library of Congress Cataloging in Publication Data
Main entry under title:

Letters in American history.

1. United States—History—Sources. 2. American letters. I. Lang, H. Jack, 1904–
E173.L49 1982   973   82-11747
ISBN: 0-517-54795-3
ISBN: 0-517-54796-1 (pbk.)

10 9 8 7 6 5 4 3 2 1
First Edition

To my wife,
Frances Wise Lang,
whose understanding patience while I
was writing and thinking about this
book was beyond the call of connubial duty

CONTENTS

ACKNOWLEDGMENTS

The editor gratefully acknowledges the valued assistance of Lewis Affelder, president of The Wolf Envelope Company, Cleveland, Ohio, and John Mahler, president of The Wolf Detroit Envelope Company, publishers of *The Wolf Magazine of Letters*, edited for forty-seven years by H. Jack Lang, from which the majority of the letters in this book have been selected. My gratitude also to Nannie Larkins, for aid in research; John A. Lang, of the University of California; Wesley C. Williams, owner of the Publix Book Mart, Cleveland, Ohio; and Harriet Bell, senior editor of Harmony Books.

SYNOPTIC INTRODUCTION

L ETTERS FURNISH THE raw material for the writing of history and sometimes even influence the course of events. Yet unlike written history, letters breathe with vitality and realism. They give a sense of living presence—a feeling almost of being a participant—as we read the words of those who played principal roles in the exciting times of the past.

This one-of-a-kind selection, from many thousands of letters written by our countrymen, was chosen for its drama, inspiration, and human interest, with particular emphasis on the unique and unusual.

As the editor of a magazine of letters for forty-seven years, I have applied what I call the "Well, I'll be damned" test. Unless the letter should bring such an astonished reaction from the reader, it was not deemed worthy of publication in the magazine. The same criterion has been applied to this collection of letters.

Take, for example, some of the strangest coincidences in America's history. John Adams's second son, Charles, died an alcoholic on skid row, while another son, John Quincy, lived to be president. Both Thomas Jefferson and John Adams died on July 4, 1826, while the fiftieth anniversary of the Declaration of Independence was being celebrated. Five years later, James Madison died on July 4. On that date in 1863, Vicksburg surrendered to Grant, and Lee was defeated at Gettysburg.

Since 1840, every president elected in a year ending in a zero died before his term of office was completed. All of these startling, chance events in the annals of our country are vividly described in letters of the time.

Included are many instances of moral and physical courage. Outstanding among the former is the letter of Josiah Quincy to his outraged father, telling why he was morally bound to act as counsel to the Redcoats in the Boston Massacre. Dr. Rush's letter recalls the courage of the signers of the Declaration of Independence, who were signing their "own death warrants." Although lesser known, Caesar Rodney's midnight ride over storm-flooded roads to make, as he thought, the Declaration unanimous, was a feat to compare with the ride of Paul Revere.

Among other heroic acts described in letters fraught with drama are Presley O'Bannon's march along the shores to Tripoli, William Barret Travis's last stand at the Alamo, as well as Colonel McAuliffe's defiant refusal to surrender when surrounded by the Germans in the Battle of the Bulge.

Epistles triumphant commemorate some of the most thrilling episodes in American history. Ethan Allen elatedly writes of the dramatic capture of Fort Ticonderoga. John Adams is "transported with enthusiasm" in announcing the signing of the Declaration of Independence, "the greatest question . . . ever was [or] will be decided among men." Congressional President Thomas McKean presents to George Washington the "Thanks of the United States in Congress assembled" for his conquest of Cornwallis and the British at Yorktown. Dr. Walter Reed heralds his discovery of the cure for deadly yellow fever in an 1800 New Year's letter to his wife. Harry Truman, on his first night in the White House, proclaims the surrender of Germany "some birthday present."

Then there are letters of loyal patriots who declined honors offered by their admirers, believing such symbols of glory contrary to the ideals of their country. George Washington, in his brusque letter to Colonel Nichola, rejected the offer of a crown; Andrew Jackson flatly refused to have a Roman sarcophagus brought from Jerusalem for his burial; Theodore Roosevelt sadly told his son why he could not in good conscience accept the Nobel prize money. Less seriously, when a new town in Massachusetts was named after Benjamin Franklin and asked him to send a bell for a steeple to be erected in his honor, wily Ben wrote that he preferred sense to sound and sent books instead of a bell; and six Iroquois Indian nations politely declined an invitation to have their braves educated at Williamsburg College, because the school could not teach them to be good runners or how to "kill an Enemy."

Letters of women have been regarded as superior for the verve and fluency of their rhetoric. Among the finest are Abigail

Adams's inspirational words to her husband upon his election as president; Dolley Madison's dramatic account of her narrow escape from Washington before it was burned by the British; stalwart Elizabeth Jackson's homily to her son Andrew, before she died from "prison fever"; and Anne Morrow Lindbergh's eloquent greeting to her famous husband returning from the Pacific Theater in World War II.

Among women pioneers who set feminist firsts are Deborah Gannett, who fought in the American Revolution disguised as a man, the first woman American soldier; and Edith Galt Wilson, often called the first lady president because she devotedly served as surrogate to her helplessly ill husband. The first aviatrix to fly solo across the Atlantic, Amelia Earhart, disappeared in an attempted flight around the world. "Even though I have lost, the adventure was worthwhile," she wrote in a letter found by her mother.

Some letters give new and revealing insight into the character of the writer, as for instance Alexander Hamilton's farewell to his wife before his fatal duel with Aaron Burr; William Tecumseh Sherman's testamentary letter proving that he meant what he said when he wrote "War is Hell"; Robert E. Lee's mental anguish in deciding to fight against his country; Dwight Eisenhower's animated defense of hanging Robert E. Lee's picture in the Oval Office; pacifist Albert Einstein's reasons for urging President Franklin Roosevelt to make the atom bomb; and Gerald Ford's explanation to critics of his reasons for pardoning Richard Nixon.

Of interest in the current wave of terrorism and assassinations is John F. Kennedy's humor, commenting on the fatal twenty-year presidential cycle, not knowing he was destined not to break the chain; a shocked Charles Eliot speaking for the whole nation in expressing his horror at Lincoln's tragic assassination; and the distorted thinking of assassins as revealed in a letter of Charles Guiteau, who killed James A. Garfield, and in a threatening message from Lee Harvey Oswald, who fatally shot John F. Kennedy.

There are minority Americans, faced with prejudice and oppression, who brought honor to their race and to their country. When most Japanese-Americans were being interned after Pearl Harbor, Hashime Saito fought in Italy with a Japanese-American regiment, "the most decorated unit in American history." There is Lyndon Johnson's antiracist act of burying a Mexican-American soldier in Arlington Cemetery with full military honors. A Cherokee Indian mother who had lost two sons in the Korean War bravely permitted her surviving boy to be retransferred from a desk job to the fighting front. And a thirteen-year-old black son of an air force sergeant, believing that helping others leads to peace, starts a movement to provide massive medical supplies for Albert Schweitzer in equatorial Africa.

Also included is a miscellany of correspondence, some known, some newly discovered, such as Roosevelt's request to a future president in 1956 to honor Colin P. Kelly, Jr., the first American hero to die in World War II, by appointing his son to West Point, which Dwight Eisenhower did not forget to do. An officer in the same war, every Christmas, sent the parents of a sergeant who had died saving his life an unsigned card saying, "I, too, have not forgotten." In his last letter he promised to take very special care of the sergeant's younger brother Eddie, who had just joined his company. And there are Communist Russia's letter to Herbert Hoover pledging eternal friendship to America for saving the lives of millions of starving Soviet peasants, and Jimmy Carter's letter on the Voyager space ship addressed to civilizations unknown.

Novel indeed is the preinflation letter written in 1962 by the president of Union College, apologizing to Noah Webster for the college's failure to acknowledge Webster's offer, a century and a half ago, of 50¢ for every thousand volumes of his *Spelling Book*, which eventually sold 100 million copies. More humorous is the bill sent to the British Exchequer by the rector of St. Peter's Church for $18, with 6 percent interest compounded annually for 183 years totaling $769,565.96, to pay for a fence destroyed by the Redcoats during the Revolution. And there is the letter from E. I. DuPont acknowledging the receipt of 32¢ in full payment for operating the Manhattan Nuclear Project.

Represented, too, are some of America's most familiar authors.

John Howard Payne, who wrote "Home Sweet Home," tells that he never had a home. Henry Thoreau announces that he has a library of 900 volumes, more than 700 of which he wrote himself. Most eloquent of all is Mark Twain's letter to Walt Whitman on his birthday, rhapsodizing on Whitman's seventy years as the "greatest in the world's history."

Together these letters compose an unforgettable anthem of words to remember. Their felicity of expression and the dramatic events that inspired them resound throughout history, a thrilling diapason of the American spirit.

—H. Jack Lang

LETTERS IN
AMERICAN HISTORY

Josiah Quincy, Jr.'s Testament to Justice

THE BOSTON MASSACRE TRIALS

The first real blood shed in the American Revolution was when five Americans were killed in the Boston Massacre in 1770. An aroused citizenry seized the British captain and eight soldiers involved and charged them with murder. Feelings ran so high against the accused Redcoats that most competent attorneys did not dare to defend them.

In desperation, the British approached the young lawyer Josiah Quincy, Jr. Only twenty-six years old, a recent graduate of Harvard, and firm in the belief of justice for all, Quincy said he would take the case, but only if the highly respected John Adams would serve with him as counsel.

Hearing of his son's decision, Josiah Quincy, Sr., hurried off a letter: "Good God! Is it possible [that you would become] an advocate for those criminals who are charged with the murder of their fellow-citizens?" In his reply, young Quincy reminded his father: "Let such be told, Sir, that these criminals, charged with murder, are not yet legally proved guilty, and therefore, however criminal, are entitled by the laws of God and man, to all legal counsel and aid . . . ."

John Adams, fully aware of the sacrifices involved, unhesitatingly agreed to take the case.

In the trial, the captain and all but two of the soldiers were found not guilty. The two who were convicted of manslaughter immediately pleaded "benefit of clergy"—under an old English law. An attendant brought in a hot iron and each was branded on his thumb and then released.

Quincy's courageous reply to his indignant father remains one of the finest testaments to the principles of justice.

Josiah Quincy, Sr., to Josiah Quincy, Jr.

Braintree, March 22,
1770.

My Dear Son,

I am under great affliction, at hearing the bitterest reproaches uttered against you, for having become an advocate for those criminals who are charged with the murder of their fellow-citizens. Good God! Is it possible? I will not believe it.

Just before I returned home from Boston, I knew, indeed, that on the day those criminals were committed to prison, a sergeant had inquired for you at your brother's house,—but I had no apprehension that it was possible an application would be made to you to undertake their defence. Since then I have been told that you have actually engaged for Captain Preston;—and I have heard the severest reflections made upon the occasion, by men who had just before manifested the highest esteem for you, as one designed to be a saviour of your country.

I must own to you, it has filled the bosom of your aged and infirm parent with anxiety and distress, lest it should not only prove true, but destructive of your reputation and interest; and I repeat, I will not believe it, unless it be confirmed by your own mouth, or under your own hand.

Your anxious and distressed parent,

Josiah Quincy.

Josiah Quincy, Jr., to Josiah Quincy, Sr.

Boston, March 26, 1770.

Honoured Sir,

I have little leisure, and less inclination either to know, or to take notice, of those ignorant slanderers, who have dared to utter their "bitter reproaches" in your hearing against me, for having become an advocate for criminals charged with murder . . . .

Let such be told, Sir, that these criminals, charged with murder, <u>are not yet legally proved guilty,</u> and therefore, however criminal, are entitled, by the laws of God and man, to all legal counsel and aid; that my duty as a man obliged me to undertake; that my duty as a lawyer strengthened the obligation; that from abundant caution, I at first declined being engaged; that after the best advice, and most mature deliberation had determined my judgment, I waited on Captain Preston, and told him that I would afford him my assistance . . . . I dare affirm, that you, and this whole people will one day REJOICE, that I became an advocate for the aforesaid "criminals," <u>charged</u> with the murder of our fellow-citizens.

I never harboured the expectation, nor any great desire, that all men should speak well of me . . . .

There are honest men in all sects,—I wish their approbation—there are wicked bigots in all parties,—I abhor them.

I am, truly and affectionately,

your son,
Josiah Quincy, Jun.

COLLEGE EDUCATION IS NOT FOR INDIANS

IT MAKES THEM "BAD RUNNERS"

I n 1774, the Virginia Colony invited six Indian nations (The Iroquois Confederacy) to send six of their young braves to be educated at Williamsburg College. The Redskins politely declined, explaining that this kind of education made them "bad Runners" and "ignorant of every means of living in the Woods." Instead they countered with an invitation to the gentlemen of Virginia to send them a dozen of their sons whom they would instruct in ways that would "make Men of them."

Greetings!

We know that you highly esteem the kind of learning taught in Colleges, and that the Maintenance of our young Men, while with you, would be very expensive to you. We are convinc'd, therefore, that you mean to do us Good by your Proposal; and we thank you heartily. But you, who are wise, must know that different Nations have different Conceptions of things; and you will therefore not take it amiss, if our Ideas of this kind of Education happen not to be the same with yours. We have had some Experience of it. Several of our Young People were formerly brought up at the Colleges of the Northern Provinces; they were instructed in all your Sciences; but, when they came back to us, they were bad Runners, ignorant of every means of living in the Woods, unable to bear either Cold or Hunger, knew neither how to build a Cabin, take a Deer, or kill an Enemy, spoke our Language imperfectly, were therefore neither fit for Hunters, Warriors, nor Counsellors, they were totally good for nothing. We are, however, not the less oblig'd by your kind Offer, tho' we decline accepting it; and, to show our grateful Sense of it, if the Gentlemen of Virginia will send us a Dozen of their Sons, we will take care of their Education; instruct them in all we know, and make Men of them.

THE SIX INDIAN
NATIONS

FORT TICONDEROGA SURRENDERS

TO ETHAN ALLEN AND HIS
GREEN MOUNTAIN BOYS

After the Boston Massacre in 1770, fighting broke out at Lexington, Concord, Bunker Hill (correctly, Breed's Hill), and near Lake Champlain in 1775, before the Declaration *of Independence. One of the most dramatic victories for the colonists was the capture by Ethan Allen and his Green Mountain Boys of the British Fort Ticonderoga, "in the name of Jehovah and the Continental Congress," elatedly described by Allen in his letter to the Massachusetts Council.*

10th day of May, 1775.

To the Massachusetts Council,
Gentlemen:

I have to inform you, with pleasure unfelt before, that on the break of day of the tenth of May, 1775, by the order of the General Assembly of the Colony of Connecticut, I took the Fortress of Ticonderoga by storm. The soldiery was composed of about one hundred Green Mountain Boys and near fifty veteran soldiers from the Province of Massachusetts Bay. The latter was under command of Colonel James Easton, who behaved with great zeal and fortitude—not only in council, but in the assault. The soldiery behaved with such resistless fury, that they so terrified the King's troops, that they durst not fire on their assailants, and our soldiery was agreeably disappointed. The soldiery behaved with uncommon rancour when they leaped into the Fort; and it must be confessed, that the Colonel has greatly contributed to the taking of that fortress, as well as John Brown, Esq., attorney at law, who was also an able counsellor, and was personally in the attack. I expect the colonies will maintain this fort. As to the cannon and war-like stores, I hope they may serve the cause of liberty instead of tyranny, and I humbly implore your assistance in immediately assisting the Government of Connecticut in establishing a garrison in the reduced premises. Colonel Easton will inform you at large. From, gentlemen, your most obedient, humble servant,

Ethan Allen

"You Are Now My Enemy— and I Am Yours"

BENJAMIN FRANKLIN'S LETTER THAT WAS NEVER SENT

I n his early years Benjamin Franklin was an Anglophile and once considered moving permanently to England. He spent more than twenty years there, many as a delegate, promoting the cause of the colonies. As the king's policies grew more oppressive, Franklin's affection turned to antagonism.

Appalled by the bloodshed in the Boston Massacre and the battles of Lexington and Concord, Franklin penned this caustic note to his old friend, the British printer and publisher of Samuel Johnson's Dictionary, William Strahan. Franklin wisely decided not to send it and the two men remained warm friends. Among famous letters written but not sent, it ranks with Lincoln's letter to General Meade, who failed to follow up his victory at Gettysburg by pursuing Lee and possibly ending the war.

Philadelphia, July 5, 1775

Mr. Strahan,

You are a Member of Parliament, and one of that Majority which has doomed my Country to Destruction—

You have begun to burn our Towns and murder our People— Look upon your hands! They are stained with the Blood of your Relations! You and I were long Friends—You are now my Enemy—and

I am
Yours,
B. Franklin

23

John Adams Would Celebrate July Second

"THE MOST MEMORABLE EPOCHA IN THE HISTORY OF AMERICA"

From the State House in Philadelphia, John Adams wrote exuberantly to his wife, Abigail, that July second "will be celebrated by succeeding generations as the great anniversary festival."

On that second day of July, Richard Henry Lee's resolution, "that these United Colonies are, of a right ought to be free and independent States," was approved by Congress. John Adams had delivered a stirring speech in support of it.

But it was the adoption two days later of the official Declaration of Independence, written by the talented young Thomas Jefferson, that led to July fourth's commemoration as Independence Day. It took the place of Massacre Day, which had been observed in several of the colonies until that time.

3 July 1776

My Dear,

Yesterday the greatest question was decided which ever was debated in America, and a greater, perhaps, never was nor will be decided among men. The second day of July 1776 will be the most memorable epocha in the history of America. I am apt to believe that it will be celebrated by succeeding generations as the great anniversary festival. It ought to be commemorated as the day of deliverance by solemn acts of devotion to God Almighty. It ought to be solemnized with pomp and parade, with shows, games, sports, guns, bells, bonfires, and illuminations, from one end of this continent to the other from this time forward forevermore.

You will think me transported with enthusiasm, but I am not. I am well aware of the toil and blood and treasure that it will cost us to maintain this Declaration and support and defend these States. Yet, through all the gloom, I can see the rays of ravishing light and glory. I can see that the end is more than worth all the means. And that posterity will triumph in that day's transaction, even although we should rue it, which I trust in God we shall not.

Yours,
John Adams

CAESAR RODNEY'S MIDNIGHT RIDE

AS DRAMATIC AS THE RIDE OF PAUL REVERE

V oting for independence was a hard choice for members of the Continental Congress. Many still harbored an affinity for Great Britain. Others were fearful for the effect on their careers and the fate of their families.

John Dickinson of Pennsylvania opposed the Declaration of Independence in these emotion-charged words, "I had rather forfeit popularity forever than vote away the blood and happiness of my countrymen." His views were echoed by some representatives of other colonies.

The Delaware delegation was divided. Thomas McKean was in favor, but George Read was adamantly opposed. Caesar Rodney, the third member, had been delayed, but rode all night through darkness, lightning, and thunder and arrived in time to cast his affirmative vote, without which the declaration would not have been unanimous. Rodney's ride, which he relates in his letter to his brother, might be considered as vital to the Revolution as Paul Revere's.

July 4, 1776

Dear Brother,

I arrived in Congress (tho detained by Thunder and Rain) time Enough to give my Voice in the matter of Independence—It is determined by the Thirteen United Colonies, without even one

25

decenting Colony*—We have now Got through with the Whole of the declaration, and Ordered it to be printed, so that you will soon have the pleasure of seeing it—Hand-bills of it will be printed and sent to Armies, Cities, County Towns &c. To be published or rather proclamed in form— . . .

Caesar

*Apparently Rodney did not know that the New York delegates did not vote for independence until ten days later.

BRITAIN'S HESSIAN MERCENARIES

⎯⎯⎯⎯

ARE MORE VALUABLE DEAD THAN ALIVE

T he German prince Count de Schaumburg supplied Hessian soldiers to fight for England in the days of Bunker Hill. Paid by Britain at the rate of thirty guineas for each dead Hessian (and pressed for funds to meet the costs of his petty, brilliant court, the expenses of his recent visit to the Riviera, and the coming season of Italian opera), he dispatched this letter to his commander in America, hoping to fatten the royal treasury.

General, Baron Hohenhorf:

I am about to send to you some new recruits. Don't economize them. Remember glory before all things. Glory is true wealth. There is nothing degrades the soldier like the love of money. He must care only for honour and reputation, but this reputation must be acquired in the midst of dangers. A battle gained without costing the conqueror any blood is an inglorious success, while the conquered cover themselves with glory by perishing with their arms in their hands. Do you remember that of the 300 Lacedaemonians who defended the defile of Thermopylae, not one returned? How happy should I be could I say the same of my brave Hessians!

February, 1777.   Count de Schaumburg

Washington Becomes Commander-in-Chief

✑

DESPITE SOME RESERVATIONS

T wo days before writing this letter to his wife, Martha, whom
he affectionately called Patsy, George Washington
acknowledged, to the president of the Continental Congress,
his appointment as commander-in-chief. Although grateful of the "high
honor," Washington added, "I do not think myself equal to the
command I am honored with."

He then explained to his "dear Patsy" why he reluctantly felt compelled to accept.

Philadelphia, 18 June,
1775

My Dearest,—

I am now set down to write to you on a subject which fills me
with inexpressible concern, and this concern is greatly aggra-
vated and increased when I reflect upon the uneasiness I know it
will give you. It has been determined in Congress that the whole
army raised for the defense of the American cause shall be put
under my care, and that it is necessary for me to proceed
immediately to Boston to take upon me the command of it.

You may believe me, my dear Patsy, when I assure you, in the
most solemn manner, that, so far from seeking this appointment,
I have used every endeavor in my power to avoid it, not only from
my unwillingness to part with you and the family, but from a
consciousness of its being a trust too great for my capacity, and
that I should enjoy more real happiness in one month with you at
home, than I have the most distant prospect of finding abroad, if
my stay were to be seven times seven years . . . .

It was utterly out of my power to refuse this appointment
without exposing my character to such censures as would have

reflected dishonor upon myself and given pain to my friends.

As life is always uncertain and common prudence dictates to every man the necessity of settling his temporal concerns while it is in his power, and while the mind is calm and undisturbed, I have, since I came to this place . . . got Colonel Pendleton to draught a will for me. . . . The provisions made for you in case of my death will, I hope, be agreeable.

I shall add nothing more . . . but . . . assure you that I am with the most unfeigned regard, my dear Patsy, your affectionate, &c.

George W.

ELIZABETH JACKSON'S ADVICE TO HER SON ANDREW

✒∕∾∾

BEFORE SHE DIED OF "PRISON FEVER"

*I*n 1765, Elizabeth Jackson left her home in Carrickfergus, Ireland, for the Waxhaws Settlement in the Carolinas. After two weary years in this pioneer community, her husband, Andrew, died. Widowed, with two small sons and pregnant with a third, she gave birth to a lively redheaded infant, whom she called Andrew after his father.

In 1780, when the Revolution came to the Waxhaws, the three young sons fought with the patriots against the hated British and the Tories. After one bloody skirmish, the elder boy, Hugh, died of exposure. Following another encounter, Robert and the thirteen-year-old Andrew were captured.

In the cramped, unsanitary quarters in which they were confined by the British, smallpox soon broke out and both brothers were stricken. Dangerously ill, they were released to their mother, who hurried to their bedside and took them on the long, exhausting journey home.

Robert soon died, but with Elizabeth's diligent care, Andrew survived.

When the crisis was past, the intrepid Mrs. Jackson took the long road to Charleston, where she had heard more American prisoners, on British prison ships, were in desperate need of nursing care. She served them devotedly until she, herself, contracted "prison fever" and in a few days succumbed. In her remaining hours she sent this testament to her soon-to-be orphaned son, later destined to be our seventh president.

Dear Andrew:

If I should not see you again I wish you to remember and treasure up some things I have already said to you: in this world you will have to make your own way. To do that you must have friends. You can make friends by being honest, and you can keep them by being steadfast. You must keep in mind that friends worth having will in the long run expect as much from you as they give to you.

To forget an obligation or be ungrateful for a kindness is a base crime—not merely a fault or a sin but an actual crime. Men guilty of it sooner or later must suffer the penalty.

In personal conduct always be polite, but never obsequious. No one will respect you more than you esteem yourself. Avoid quarrels as long as you can without yielding to imposition. But sustain your manhood always . . . .

Never wound the feelings of others. If ever you have to vindicate your feelings or defend your honor, do it calmly. If angry at first, wait till your wrath cools before you proceed.

Love,
Mother

THE PRESIDENT OF THE CONTINENTAL CONGRESS

⌒⌒⌒

HAILS THE SURRENDER OF GENERAL CORNWALLIS

When George Washington won the last decisive battle of the American Revolution at Yorktown, he dispatched his aide in the middle of the night to notify President Thomas McKean of the Continental Congress of the surrender of General Cornwallis.

President McKean, who had voted for independence with Caesar Rodney, expressed the gratitude and admiration of the Congress and the country for Washington's great victory.

Philadelphia
October 31, 1781

His Excellency General Washington
Sir,

It affords me ineffable pleasure to present to your Excellency the Thanks of the United States in Congress assembled, for the distinguished services you have rendered to your Country, and particularly for the conquest of Lord Cornwallis and the British Garrisons of York and Gloucester, and the wisdom and prudence manifested in the Capitulation.

You have herewith inclosed a copy of the Act of Congress passed on this occasion upon the 29th instant, which fully expresses the sentiments with which they are impressed by this glorious event.

Words fail me when I attempt to bestow my small tribute of thanks and praise to a Character so eminent for wisdom, courage and patriotism, & one who appears to be no less the Favorite of Heaven than of his country; I shall only therefore beg you to be assured that you are held in the most grateful remembrance, and with a peculiar veneration, by all the wise and good in these United States.

That you may long possess this happiness, that you may be enabled speedily to annihilate the British power in America, which you have so effectually broken by this last capital blow, that you may be ever hailed the Deliverer of your Country, and enjoy every blessing Heaven can bestow in the sincere and ardent Prayer of one, who professes himself to be, with every sentiment of regard and all possible attachment,

> Sir,
> Your Excellency's most
> obedient and devoted
> humble Servant
> Thos McKean, President

GEORGE WASHINGTON REFUSES
A CROWN

HE VIEWS THE IDEA OF BEING KING
WITH ABHORRENCE

O*n more than one occasion George Washington had troubles with his officers. The mutinous "Conway Cabal" took place early in the Revolution. Washington was defeated at Brandywine and Germantown. General Horatio Gates was given credit for the first important American victory over Burgoyne at Saratoga. General Thomas Conway led a plot to replace Washington as commander-in-chief with General Gates. Word of the plan reached Washington, who quickly put a stop to the conspiracy.*

In later years, a group of officers were convinced that the United States could not survive as a nation under a republican form of government. Their leader, Colonel Nichola, wrote to Washington suggesting the establishment of a monarchy with Washington as king. In his reply, America's first president firmly stated: "I must view with abhorrence. . . [the proposal] which to me seems big with the greatest mischiefs that can befall my Country."

Newburgh May 22 '82

Sir,

With a mixture of great surprise & astonishment I have read with attention the Sentiments you have submitted to my perusal.—Be assured Sir, no occurrence in the course of the War, has given me more painful sensations than your information of there being such ideas existing in the Army as you have expressed, & I must view with abhorrence, and reprehend with severety—For the present, the communication of them will rest in my own bosom, unless some further agitation of the matter shall make a disclosure necessary—

I am much at a loss to conceive what part of my conduct could have given encouragement to an address which to me seems big with the greatest mischiefs that can befall my Country.—If I am not deceived in the knowledge of myself, you could not have found a person to whom your schemes are more disagreeable—at the same time in justice to my own feeling I must add, that no man possesses a more sincere wish to see ample justice done to the Army than I do, and as far as my powers & influence, in a constitution may extend, they shall be employed to the utmost of my abilities to effect it, should there be any occasion—Let me conjure you then, if you have any regard for your Country—concern for yourself or posterity—or respect for me, to banish these thoughts from your mind, & never communicate, as from yourself, or any one else, a sentiment of the like nature.—

With esteem I am Sir
Yr. Most Obed Ser
G. Washington

Col Nichola

"Sense Being Preferable to Sound"

❦

FRANKLIN SENDS BOOKS INSTEAD OF A BELL

A new town in Massachusetts, which was to be named Franklin after the famous patriot, asked him to send a bell for a steeple to be erected in his honor. Believing sense to be preferable to sound, Benjamin Franklin asked Dr. Price to obtain some books to be sent as a gift instead of a bell. Today there are thirty-one communities in the United States named Franklin—and twenty-eight named Washington.

Passy, March 18, 1785.

My Dear Friend:

My nephew, Mr. Williams, will have the honour of delivering you this line. It is to request from you a list of a few good books to the value of about twenty-five pounds, such as are most proper to inculcate principles of sound religion and just government. A new town in the State of Massachusetts having done me the honour of naming itself after me, and proposing to build a steeple to their meeting-house if I would give them a bell, I have advised the sparing themselves the expense of a steeple at present, and that they would accept of books instead of a bell, sense being preferable to sound. These are therefore intended as the commencement of a little parochial library for the use of a society of intelligent, respectable farmers such as our country people generally consist of. Besides your own works, I would only mention, on the recommendation of my sister, Stennet's Discourses on Personal Religion, which may be one book of the number, if you know it and approve of it.

With the highest esteem and respect, I am ever, my dear friend, yours most affectionately. . . .

B. Franklin

PARDON MY REVOLUTION

❦

G. WASHINGTON BELATEDLY REPLIES TO THE EMPEROR OF MOROCCO

George Washington explains to Mohammed III of Morocco that a revolution and the creation of a new country have delayed his sending his appreciation for the emperor's friendship to the United States. Washington also thanks the emperor for his efforts to persuade the Bashaws of Tunis and Tripoli [Libya] to stop demanding tribute for American ships captured by the Barbary pirates. The Bashaws ignored the requests and continued to seize the ships and hold the sailors as hostage until the United States declared war, and set the stage for the marine Presley O'Bannon's heroic exploits.

Mohammed III's descendant, Hassan II, the present emperor of Morocco, was one of the few Arab leaders who did not oppose Anwar Sadat's peace visit to Israel.

City of New York the first
day of December 1789

Great and magnanimous Friend,

Since the date of the letter, which the late Congress, by their President, addressed to your Imperial Majesty, the United States of America, have thought proper to change their government, and to institute a new one, agreeable to the Constitution, of which I have the honor of herewith inclosing a copy. The time necessarily employed in this arduous task, and the derangements occasioned by so great, though peaceable a Revolution, will apologize, and account for your Majesty's not having received those regular advices, and marks of attention from the United States, which the Friendship and Magnanimity of your conduct towards them afforded reason to expect.

The United States, having unanimously appointed me to the supreme executive authority in this nation, your Majesty's letter of the 17th of August, 1788, which, by reason of the dissolution of the late government, remained unanswered, has been delivered to me. I have also received the letters which your Imperial Majesty has been so kind as to write, in favor of the United States, to the Bashaws of Tunis and Tripoli, and I present to you the sincere acknowledgments and thanks of the United States for this important mark of your friendship for them.

We greatly regret that the hostile disposition of those regencies towards this nation, who have never injured them, is not to be removed on terms in our power to comply with. Within our territories there are no mines either of gold or silver, and this young nation, just recovering from the waste and desolation of a long war, have not, as yet, had time to acquire riches by agriculture and commerce. But our soil is bountiful and our people industrious, and we have reason to flatter ourselves that we shall gradually become useful to our friends. . . .

May the Almighty bless your Imperial Majesty, our great and magnanimous Friend, with His constant guidance and protection.

G. Washington

Abigail to John Adams on His Inauguration

"To Give Thy Honors to the Day"

On the day of his inauguration as second president of the United States, John Adams received this message of inspiration from his devoted wife. Abigail offered prayers to the Almighty for helping John deal with the problems of a new nation and the troubles overseas, where war with France was imminent. Her mastery of words demonstrated why Abigail Adams was not only First Lady of the land but first lady of letter writers of all time.

"The sun is dressed in brightest beams,
To give thy honors to the day."

And may it prove an auspicious prelude to each ensuing season. You have this day to declare yourself head of a nation. "And now, O lord, my God, thou hast made thy servant ruler over the people. Give unto him an understanding heart, that he may know how to go out and come in before this great people; that he may discern between good and bad. For who is able to judge this thy so great a people?" were the words of a royal sovereign; and not less applicable to him who is invested with the chief magistracy of a nation, though he wear not a crown, nor the robes of royalty.

My thoughts and my meditations are with you, though personally absent; and my petitions to Heaven are, that "the things which make for peace may not be hidden from your eyes." My feelings are not those of pride or ostentation, upon the occasion. They are solemnized by a sense of the obligations, the important trusts, and numerous duties connected with it. That you may be enabled to discharge them with honor to yourself, with justice and impartiality to your country, and with satisfaction to this great people, shall be the daily prayer of your

A. A.

JEFFERSON WRITES DR. RUSH ON THE "SCOURGE" OF YELLOW FEVER

WALTER REED CONQUERS THE DISEASE 100 YEARS LATER

D r. Benjamin Rush was a courageous hero of the yellow fever plague that devastated Philadelphia in 1793, though he was controversial because of the radical purges and bleedings he *prescribed for those stricken. More than 5,000 died, many more contracted the disease, and thousands fled in fear from the city.*

Philadelphia was then the capital of the new country. President Washington and his cabinet, including Thomas Jefferson as secretary of state, moved their headquarters to Germantown, and Congress adjourned until the epidemic ceased.

In the next few years seven more great plagues hit Philadelphia and spread to many towns and cities throughout the country.

In 1800, before he became the first president to be inaugurated in the new capital of Washington, D.C., Jefferson, in a letter to Dr. Rush, hoped that the deadly plagues would "discourage the growth of great cities."

Later in this same letter, Jefferson proclaimed his famous dictum: "I have sworn upon the altar of God, eternal hostility against every form of tyranny over the mind of man."

One hundred years later, in an army barracks in Cuba, Dr. Walter Reed conducted an experiment on a young Ohioan named Moran. It provided the proof Dr. Reed had sought that yellow fever could be transmitted only by the Aedes aegyptic mosquito. This led to the elimination of the dreaded plague and made possible the completion of the Panama Canal.

On New Year's Eve, 1900, Dr. Reed heralded the discovery in a letter to his wife.

Thomas Jefferson to Dr. Benjamin Rush

Monticello
September 23,1800

Dear Sir,

I have to acknowledge the receipt of your favor of August the 22d, and to congratulate you on the healthiness of your city. Still Baltimore, Norfolk and Providence admonish us that we are not clear of our new scourge. When great evils happen, I am in the habit of looking out for what good may arise from them as consolations to us, and Providence has in fact so established the order of things, as that most evils are the means of producing some good. The yellow fever will discourage the growth of great cities in our nation, and I view great cities as pestilential to the morals, the health and the liberties of man. True, they nourish some of the elegant arts, but the useful ones can thrive elsewhere, and less perfection in the others, with more health, virtue and freedom, would be my choice. . . .

Thomas Jefferson

Dr. Walter Reed to His Wife

Columbia Barracks
Quemados, Cuba
11:50 P.M., Dec. 31, 1900

My Dear:

. . . Only ten minutes of the old century remain. Here have I been sitting, reading that most wonderful book, "La Roche on Yellow Fever," written in 1853. Forty-seven years later it has been permitted to me and my assistants to lift the impenetrable veil that has surrounded the causation of this most dreadful pest of humanity and to put it on a rational and scientific basis. I thank God that this has been accomplished during the latter days of the old century. May its cure be wrought in the early days of the new! The prayer that has been mine for twenty years, that I might be permitted in some way or at some time to do something to alleviate human suffering has been granted! A thousand Happy New Years! . . . Hark, there go the twenty-four buglers in concert, all sounding "Taps" for the old year.

Walter

ABIGAIL ADAMS CONSOLES HER DAUGHTER-IN-LAW

HER ONE SON DIES AN ALCOHOLIC, ANOTHER BECOMES PRESIDENT

C*harles, the second son of John and Abigail Adams, was a constant worry to his parents. Although intelligent and attractive, he was unsuccessful at law and business and everything he tried. He lived a high life, beyond his means, and soon took to drinking. Despondent because he had squandered money entrusted to him by his brother for investment, he became an incurable alcoholic. Leaving home, he sought what shelter he could on skid row. His health deteriorated rapidly, and on December 30, 1799, he became fatally ill.*

In this letter Abigail consoles her daughter-in-law, Charles's widow Sarah, and assures her that because of her devotion to her husband she should feel no guilt. Abigail asks her to remember the good qualities of her "poor deluded son." She also sends her love to "Abbe," her granddaughter and namesake.

The letter is a fine example of Abigail's skill as a letter writer and a rare instance of history's ironies, in that one son ended his life on skid row while another, John Quincy Adams, lived to be president of the United States.

Washington December
8th 1800

My Dear Daughter

Whilst I feel as a parent, I sympathize with you as a wife, hopeing that all the frailties and offences of my dear departed son may be forgiven and buried with his mortal past.

I besought the Throne of grace that he might find mercy from his God, to the great judge of us all we must leave him, resigning our wills to the Sovereign of the universe—

From my own thoughts and reflections I trace the sorrow of your soul, and feel every pang which greives your Heart. Would to God that I could administer to you; that comfort which I stand in need of myself.

Upon your part, you have the consolation of having performed your Duty, no remembrance of any unkindness has detered your fulfilling it, even to the last distressing scene, may you be rewarded by a self approving conscience; until fatal propensities took intire possession of this poor deluded man; he was kind, and affectionate, beloved by all his acquaintance; an enemy to no one, but a favorite where ever he went, in early life no child was more tender and amiable; but neither his mind, or constitution could survive the habits he but too fatally persued, in the midst of his days, his course is stoped, and his years numbered. May I be enabled in silence to bow myself in submission to my maker, whose attributes are Mercy, as well as well as judgments. The children will be ever dear to me, may they be raised up in the way in which they should go I will supply to them as far as in my power, the parent they have lost—

The president sends his love to you and mourns with, as he has a long time for you—

I am with a respectfull remembrance to your Mother and Love to Nancy and Abbe—

My Dear Daughter
Your Affectionate
Mother
Abigail Adams

Susan is well except a
cold—sends her duty—

ALEXANDER HAMILTON'S FAREWELL TO HIS WIFE

BEFORE HIS FATAL DUEL WITH AARON BURR

T*he presidential election of 1800 ended in a tie between Thomas Jefferson and Aaron Burr. This threw the election into the House of Representatives. Hamilton considered Burr's* rival, Jefferson, the lesser of two evils. Jefferson "is by far not so dangerous a man; and he has pretension to character," Hamilton wrote. "As to Burr, there is nothing in his favor. His private character is not defended by his most partial friends. . . . He is truly the Catiline of America." With Hamilton's support, Jefferson was elected president and Burr vice-president.

Four years later, when Burr was running for the governorship of New York, Hamilton cast similar aspersions on the character of Burr. Burr challenged him to a duel. Hamilton did not approve of duels, but felt he would be dishonored if he refused. After writing this farewell letter to his wife, Hamilton met Burr on the field. Hamilton fired harmlessly into the air, but Burr's shot was fatal. The killing of this "architect of a more perfect union" was a tragic loss for America.

My dear Eliza—

This letter, my very dear Eliza, will not be delivered to you, unless I shall first have terminated my earthly career, to begin, as I humbly hope, from redeeming grace and divine mercy, a happy immortality. If it had been possible for me to have avoided the interview, my love for you and my precious children would have been alone a decisive motive. But it was not possible, without sacrifices which would have rendered me unworthy of your esteem. I need not tell you of the pangs I feel from the idea of quitting you, and exposing you to the anguish which I know you would feel. Nor could I dwell on the topic, lest it should unman me. The consolations of religion, my beloved, can alone support you; and these you have a right to enjoy. Fly to the bosom of your God, and be comforted. With my last idea I shall cherish the sweet hope of meeting you in a better world. Adieu, best of wives—best of women. Embrace all my darling children for me.

Ever Yours
AH

"TO THE SHORES OF TRIPOLI"

THE LEGEND OF PRESLEY O'BANNON, TOUGHEST OF THE TOUGH MARINES

S trangest of all the ventures of American armed forces was the capture of Derne in Libya in 1805." There began the legend of Presley O'Bannon, toughest of all the tough marines. Thence sprang the inspiration for the Leathernecks' stirring marching tune, "From the halls of Montezuma to the shores of Tripoli."

It all started in 1802 when Hamouda Bashaw of Tripoli extorted thousands of dollars in tribute for the right of U.S. ships to trade in the Mediterranean. Hard-boiled and no appeaser, General William Eaton resigned his post as U.S. emissary to the Barbary Coast rather than pay the pirates.

Three years later when war broke out with Tripoli, General Eaton rushed back to Alexandria and marched across 500 miles of searing desert with a motley force of marines, Greeks, and Arabs, including Hamet Bashaw, the rightful sovereign of Tripoli. At the gate of Derne he dispatched with a flag of truce this message to the Bey, a ruler as violent as Muammar el-Qaddafy and his modern terrorists.

Environs of Derne, April 26th.

His Excellency of the Governor of Derne.

Sir,

I want no territory. With me is advancing the legitimate Sovereign of your country—give us a passage through your city; and for the supplies of which we shall have need, you shall receive fair compensation. Let no difference of religion induce us to shed the blood of harmless men who think little and know nothing. If you are a man of liberal mind you will not balance on the propositions I offer. Hamet Bashaw pledges himself to me that you shall be established in your government. I shall see you tomorrow in a way of your choice.

Eaton

With the flag of truce came back this four-word message from the Bey: "My head or yours!"

What then ensued led to the first raising of the American flag on foreign soil. General Eaton tells how it happened in this letter to Commodore Samuel Barron.

Derne, April 29th, 1805.

Sir,

. . . I immediately put the army in motion, and advanced towards the city. . . . A detachment of six American marines, a company of 24 cannoniers, and another of 26 Greeks, including their proper officers, all under the immediate command of Lieut. O'Bannon, together with a few Arabs on foot, had a position on an eminence opposite to a considerable party of the enemy, who had taken post behind their temporary parapets and in a ravine at the S.E. quarter of the town. The Bashaw seized an old castle which overlooked the town on the S.S.W. disposing his cavalry upon the plains in the rear. A little before 2 P.M. the fire became general in all quarters where Tripolitans and Americans were opposed to each other. In three quarters of an hour the battery was silenced, but not abandoned; though most of the enemy withdrew precipitately from that quarter and joined the party opposed to the handful of Christians with me, which appeared our most vulnerable point. Unfortunately the fire of our field piece was relaxed by the rammer being shot away. The fire of the enemy's musketry became too warm, and continually augmenting. Our troops were thrown into confusion; and, undisciplined as they were, it was impossible to reduce them to order. I perceived a charge our dernier and only resort. We rushed forward against a host of savages more than ten to our one. They fled from their coverts irregularly, firing in retreat from every palm tree and partition wall in their way. At this moment I received a ball through my left wrist which deprived me of the use of the hand, and of course my rifle. Mr. O'Bannon, accompanied by Mr. Mann of Annapolis surged forward with his marines, Greeks, and such of the cannoniers as were not necessary to the management of the field piece; passed through a shower of musketry from the walls of houses; took possession of the battery; planted the American flag upon its ramparts; and turned its guns upon the enemy. . . .

Of the few Christians who fought on shore, I lost fourteen killed and wounded; three of whom are marines, one dead and another dying; the rest chiefly Greeks, who, in this little affair, well supported their ancient character. . . .

I have the honor to be, with great respect and sincere attachment,

> Sir, your very obedient
> servant,
> William Eaton

THOMAS PAINE'S
TWO-SHILLING PAMPHLET
⟨∽⟩
PROVIDED THE BATTLE CRY FOR
INDEPENDENCE

D r. Benjamin Rush was a member of the congress which on July 4, 1776, declared the colonies "Free and Independent States." In this letter he tells how the small printing shop of Robert Bell published a forty-seven-page anonymous pamphlet, for two shillings, called "Common Sense." The author was Thomas Paine, a penniless immigrant from England, whose stirring words fired the colonists' struggle for independence.

> Philadelphia, July 17th,
> 1809.

Sir,

In compliance with your request, I send you herewith, answers to your questions relative to the late Thomas Paine.

He came to Philadelphia about the year 1774, with a short letter of introduction from Dr. Franklin to one of his friends. His design was to open a school for the instruction of young ladies in several branches of knowledge, which, at that time, were seldom taught in the female schools of our country.

About the year 1775, I met him accidentally in Mr. Aitkin's

bookstore, and was introduced to him by Mr. Aitkin. . . .

When the subject of American Independence began to be agitated in conversations, I observed the publick mind to be loaded with an immense mass of prejudice and error relative to it. Something appeared to be wanting, to remove them, beyond the ordinary short and cold addresses of newspaper publications. At this time I called upon Mr. Paine and suggested to him the propriety of preparing our citizens for a perpetual separation of our country from Great Britain, by means of a work of such length as would obviate all the objections to it. He seized the idea with avidity, and immediately began his famous pamphlet in favor of that measure. He read the sheets to me at my house as he composed them. When he had finished them, I advised him to put them into the hands of Dr. Franklin, Samuel Adams, and the late Judge Wilson, assuring him, at the same time, that they all held the same opinions that he had defended. . . . No addition was made to it by Dr. Franklin, but a passage was struck out, or omitted in printing it, which I conceived to be one of the most striking in it. It was the following—"A greater absurdity cannot be conceived of, than three millions of people running to their sea coast every time a ship arrives from London, to know what portion of liberty they should enjoy."

A title only was wanted for this pamphlet before it was committed to the press. Mr. Paine proposed to call it "plain truth." I objected to it and suggested the title of "Common Sense." This was instantly adopted and nothing now remained, but to find a printer who had boldness enough to publish it. At this time there was a certain Robert Bell, an intelligent Scotch bookseller and printer in Philadelphia, whom I knew to be as high toned as Mr. Paine upon the subject of American Independence. I mentioned the pamphlet to him, and he at once consented to run the risk of publishing it. The author and the printer were immediately brought together, and "Common Sense" bursted from the press of the latter in a few days with an effect which has rarely been produced by types and paper in any age or country. . . .

From, sir,
Yours, Respectfully,
Benjn. Rush

DR. RUSH RECALLS THE COURAGE OF THE SIGNERS

CO

THEY WERE SIGNING THEIR "OWN DEATH WARRANTS"

W hereas *"the military men, and particularly one of them, ran away with all the glory of the day," the patriots who signed their names to the Declaration of Independence displayed no less courage. They knew they would be marked men by the British and Tories who swore vengeance and persecution of the "rebels" for their treason. The British ravished the 1,000-acre farm of Lewis Morton of New York and drove his family into exile; Richard Stockton of New Jersey was jailed, nearly starved, and his estate, including the finest library in the colonies, was destroyed. Others were subjected to severer punishment. John Martin of Pennsylvania, abused by his former friends, had a physical breakdown and died within a few months; Francis Lewis's estate was seized and his wife imprisoned and mistreated until she passed away; John Hart's New Jersey farm was pillaged and he was forced to leave his dying wife. Many who declared themselves for Independence faced cruel persecution and some were signing their "own death warrants," as Dr. Benjamin Rush wrote in his letter to John Adams.*

July 20, 1811

Dear Old Friend,

The 4th of July has been celebrated in Philadelphia in the manner I expected. The military men, and particularly one of them, ran away with all the glory of the day. Scarcely a word was said of the solitude and labors and fears and sorrows and sleepless nights of the men who projected, proposed, defended, and subscribed the Declaration of Independence. Do you recollect your memorable speech upon the day on which the vote was taken? Do you recollect the pensive and awful silence which pervaded the house when we were called up, one after another, to the table of the President of Congress to subscribe what was believed by many at that time to be our own death warrants? The silence and the gloom of the morning were interrupted, I well recollect, only for a moment by Colonel Harrison of Virginia, who said to Mr. Gerry at the table: "I shall have a great advantage over you, Mr. Gerry, when we are all hung for what we are now doing. From the size and weight of my body I shall die in a few minutes, but from the lightness of your body you will dance in the air an hour or two before you are dead." This speech procured a transient smile, but it was soon succeeded by the solemnity with which the whole business was conducted. . . .

Let us, my dear friend, console ourselves for the unsuccessful efforts of our lives to serve our fellow creatures by recollecting that we have aimed well, that we have faithfully strove to tear from their hands the instruments of death with which they were about to destroy themselves, that we have attempted to take off their fancied crowns and royal robes and to clothe them with their own proper dresses, and that we have endeavored to snatch the poisoned bowl from their lips and to replace it with pleasant and wholesome food. We shall not, I hope, lose our reward for these well-intended labors of love. . . .

Benjn. Rush

DOLLEY MADISON FLEES BEFORE WASHINGTON IS BURNED

HOW THE WHITE HOUSE GOT ITS NAME

*A*fter defeating a hurriedly organized American militia at nearby Bladensburg, British forces entered Washington on August 24, 1814. They arrived at the presidential mansion just in time to enjoy an uneaten dinner prepared for President Madison and forty guests. Then the British General Ross ordered all the furniture to be piled up and the mansion set on fire. Soon the half-finished Capitol and all other public buildings were ablaze.

Amid all of the panic, the president's wife, Dolley Madison, wrote her sister, telling of her last-minute escape. In her hurry, she left behind many of her possessions but refused to leave without saving Gilbert Stuart's famous portrait of George Washington.

After burning the city, the British withdrew. The Madisons shortly returned to find the interior of their home burned out and the walls scorched but intact. The interior was rebuilt and the walls were painted white to cover the smoke stains. Ever since, the presidential mansion has been known as the White House.

Tuesday, August 23, 1814

Dear Sister,—

My husband left me yesterday morning to join General Winder. He inquired anxiously whether I had courage or firmness to remain in the President's house until his return on the morrow, or succeeding day, and on my assurance that I had no fear but for him, and the success of our army, he left, beseeching me to take care of myself, and of the Cabinet papers, public and private. I have since received two despatches from him, written with a pencil. The last is alarming, because he desires I should be ready at a moment's warning to enter my carriage, and leave the city; that the enemy seemed stronger than had at first been reported, and it might happen that they would reach the city with the intention of destroying it. I am accordingly ready; I have pressed as many Cabinet papers into trunks as to fill one carriage; our private property must be sacrificed, as it is impossible to procure wagons for its transportation. I am determined not to go myself until I see Mr. Madison safe, so that he can accompany me, as I hear of much hostility towards him. Disaffection stalks around us. My friends and acquaintances are all gone, even Colonel C. with his hundred, who were stationed as a guard in this inclosure. French John (a faithful servant), with his usual activity and resolution, offers to spike the cannon at the gate, and lay a train of powder, which would blow up the British, should they enter the house. To the last proposition I positively object, without being able to make him understand why all advantages in war may not be taken.

Wednesday Morning, twelve o'clock.—Since sunrise I have been turning my spy-glass in every direction, and watching with unwearied anxiety, hoping to discover the approach of my dear husband and his friends; but, alas! I can descry only groups of military, wandering in all directions, as if there was a lack of arms, or of spirit to fight for their own fireside.

Three o'clock.—Will you believe it, my sister? we have had a battle, or skirmish, near Bladensburg, and here I am still, within sound of the cannon! Mr. Madison comes not. May God protect us! Two messengers, covered with dust, come to bid me fly; but here I mean to wait for him....At this late hour a wagon has been procured, and I have had it filled with plate and the most valuable portable articles, belonging to the house. Whether it will reach its destination, the "Bank of Maryland," or fall into the hands of British soldiery, events must determine. Our kind friend, Mr. Carroll, has come to hasten my departure, and in a very bad humor with me, because I insist on waiting until the large picture of General Washington is secured, and it requires to be unscrewed from the wall. This process was found too tedious for these perilous moments; I have ordered the frame to be broken, and the canvas taken out. It is done! and the precious portrait placed in the hands of two gentlemen of New York, for safe keeping. And now, dear sister, I must leave this house, or the retreating army will make me a prisoner in it by filling up the road I am directed to take. When I shall again write to you, or where I shall be tomorrow, I cannot tell!

Dolley

THE FIRST WOMAN SOLDIER

FOUGHT IN THE AMERICAN REVOLUTION

D eborah Gannett, of Middleboro, Massachusetts, disguised as a man, enlisted in the Revolutionary army as Private Robert Shurtleff. Her sex was not discovered until she was hospitalized with fever, while serving as aide-de-camp. After her honorable discharge, she made this application for a disability pension, which was willingly granted.

Deborah Gannett has been regarded as the first woman to serve as a fighting member of the U.S. armed forces.

United States
Massachusetts District—

Deborah Gannett, of Sharon, in the county of Norfolk, and District of Massachusetts, as resident and native of the United States, and applicant for a pension from the United States, under an Act of Congress entitled an Act to provide for certain persons engaged in the land and Naval Service of the United States, in the revolutionary war, maketh oath, That she served as a private soldier, under the name of Robert Shurtleff—in the war of the revolution, upwards of two years in manner following. Viz.—Enlisted in April 1781 in the company commanded by Captain George Webb in the Massachusetts Regiment commanded then by Colonel Shepherd—and afterwards by Colonel Henry Jackson—and served in said corps in Massachusetts, and New York—until November 1783—when she was honorably discharged in writing, which discharge is lost—During the time of her service, she was at the capture of Lord Cornwallis—was wounded at Tarrytown. . . . She is in such reduced circumstances, as to require the aid of her country,—For her support—

Deborah Gannett

Massts. Dis. Sept. 14, 1818
Sworn to before Me:
Jno Davis Dis. Judge Mass. Dist.

ADAMS'S AND JEFFERSON'S LAST
LETTERS ON JULY 4, 1826
ON THE FIFTIETH ANNIVERSARY OF
INDEPENDENCE DAY

I n 1826, ceremonies were being planned throughout the country to celebrate the fiftieth anniversary of Independence Day. The citizens of Quincy, Massachusetts, invited the ailing ninety-one-year-old John Adams to join in their festivities. The mayor of Washington sent a similar invitation to the indisposed eighty-three-year-old Thomas Jefferson. In sending their regrets, both ex-presidents heralded the significance of the day.

On July 4, 1826, the very day their letters were being read to the assembled citizens, John Adams died. His last words were, "Thomas Jefferson survives." He did not know that Jefferson had died a few hours before. The deaths of both of these great patriots on the fiftieth anniversary of the Declaration of Independence is one of the strangest coincidences in the annals of America. Five years later, James Madison, the fourth president and principal author of the Constitution, also died on July 4.

John Adams to the Citizens of Quincy

Quincy, June 7, 1826

Sir,

Your letter of the 3rd Instant, written on behalf of the Committee of Arrangements, for the approaching celebration of our National Independence; inviting me to dine, on the fourth of July next, with the Citizens of Quincy, at the Town Hall, has been received with the kindest emotions. The very respectful language with which the wishes of my Fellow Townsmen have been conveyed to me, by your Committee, and the terms of affectionate regard toward me, individually demand my grateful

51

thanks, which you will please to accept and to communicate to your Colleagues of the Committee.

The present feeble state of my health will not permit me to indulge the hope of participating with more than by my best wishes in the joys and festivities and the solemn services of that day, on which will be completed the fiftieth year from its birth, the independence of the United States: A memorable epoch in the annals of the human race, destined, in future history, to form the BRIGHTEST OR THE BLACKEST PAGE according to the use or the abuse of these political institutions by which they shall, in time to come, be shaped by the human mind.

I pray you, sir, to tender, in my behalf to our fellow-citizens, my cordial thanks for their affectionate good wishes, and to be assured that I am very truly and affectionately yours and their friend and fellow-townsman,

J. Adams

Thomas Jefferson to the Mayor of Washington

Monticello
June 24, 1826

Respected Sir,

The kind invitation I received from you, on the part of the citizens of the city of Washington, to be present with them at their celebration of the fiftieth anniversary of American Independence, as one of the surviving signers of an instrument pregnant with our town, and the fate of the world, is most flattering to myself, and heightened by the honorable accompaniment proposed for the comfort of such a journey. It adds sensibly to the sufferings of sickness, to be deprived by it of a personal participation in the rejoicing of that day . . . . I should, indeed, with peculiar delight, have met and exchanged there congratulations personally with the small band, the remnant of that host of worthies, who joined with us on that day, in the bold and doubtful election we were to make for our country, between submission or the sword; and to have enjoyed with them the consolatory fact, that our fellow-citizens, after half a century of experience and prosperity, continue to approve the choice we made. May it be to the world, what I believe it will be (to some parts sooner, to others later, but finally to all), the signal of arousing men to burst the chains under which monkish ignorance and superstition had persuaded them to bind themselves, and to resume the blessings and security of self-government. . . . All eyes are opened, or opening, to the rights of man. The general spread of the light of science has already laid open to every view the palpable truth, that the mass of mankind has not been born with saddles on their backs, nor a favored few booted and spurred, ready to ride them legitimately, by the grace of God. These are grounds of hope for others. For ourselves, let the annual return of this day forever refresh our recollections of these rights, and an undiminished devotion to them. . . .

With my regret that ill health forbids me the gratification of an acceptance, be pleased to receive for yourself, and those for whom you write, the assurance of my highest respect and friendly attachment.

Th: Jefferson

VAN BUREN WARNS
ANDREW JACKSON

OF AN EVIL NEW FORM OF
TRANSPORTATION

ore than 150 years ago, before he became the first
American-born president, Martin Van Buren warned
President Andrew Jackson that an evil, new form of
transportation, called railroads, would displant canal boats. The
result, Van Buren believed, would be disruption of business, higher
unemployment, and weakening of defense.

As predicted, canals have fallen into disuse. Railroads, too, have suffered from competition by trucks and planes. But recently, service on high-speed "bullet trains" began between Lyons and Paris. Instead of "speeding" at 15 miles an hour, they travel at more than 100 miles an hour.

January 31, 1829

To: President Andrew Jackson

The canal system of this country is being threatened by the spread of a new form of transportation known as 'railroads'. The federal government must preserve the canals for the following reasons:

One. If canal boats are supplanted by 'railroads' serious unemployment will result. Captains, cooks, drivers, hostlers, repairmen and lock tenders will be left without means of livelihood, not to mention the numerous farmers now employed in growing hay for horses.

Two. Boat builders would suffer and towline, whip and harness makers would be left destitute.

Three. Canal boats are absolutely essential to the defense of the United States. In the event of the expected trouble with England, the Erie Canal would be the only means by which we could ever move the supplies so vital to waging modern war.

For the above-mentioned reasons the government should create an Interstate Commerce Commission to protect the American people from the evils of 'railroads' and to preserve the canals for posterity.

As you may well know, Mr. President, 'railroad' carriages are pulled at the enormous speed of 15 miles per hour by 'engines' which, in addition to endangering life and limb of passengers, roar and snort their way through the countryside, setting fire to crops, scaring the livestock and frightening women and children. The Almighty certainly never intended that people should travel at such breakneck speed.

Martin Van Buren
Governor of New York

*The authenticity of this letter is questionable. Some historians believe it to be apocryphal.

OLD HICKORY CARRIES OUT HIS FAMOUS TOAST

"OUR FEDERAL UNION: IT MUST BE PRESERVED"

When the tariff of 1828 protected the textile factories in the North at the expense of the consumers in the South, South Carolina refused to pay the taxes ("Nullification") and threatened to secede from the Union if forced to do so.

President Andrew Jackson, or Old Hickory, as he was called, angered and determined, promptly ordered his secretary of war to send troops on steamers to the bay of Charleston and put down with arms any attempts to nullify or secede. A compromise was reached, averting a civil war until Lincoln was elected, nearly thirty years later.

Decbr 17th 1832

My D. Sir,

I can judge from the signs of the times Nullification, & secession, or in the language of truth, <u>disunion</u> is gaining strength, and we must be prepared to act with promptness, and crush the monster in its cradle, before it matures to manhood. We must be prepared for the crisis.

The moment that we are informed that the Legislature of So Carolina has passed laws to carry her rebellious ordinance into effect which I expect tomorrow we must be prepared to act. Tenders of service is coming to me daily and from New York we can send to the bay of Charleston with steamers, such number of troops as we may please to order in four days.

We will want three Divisions of artillery, each composed of nines, twelves, & Eighteen pounders—one for the East, one for the West, and one for the center divisions. How many of these calibers, are ready for field service.

How many musketts with their compleat equipments are ready for service. How many swords & pistols & what quantity of hand ammunition for Dragoons—Brass pieces for the field, how many, & what caliber.

At as early a day as possible, I wish a report from the ordinance Department, on this subject, stating with precision, how many pieces of artillery of the caliber, are ready for the field—how many good musketts, etc etc, and at what place in depart—Secretary of War—

> yrs respectfully
> Andrew Jackson

"REMEMBER THE ALAMO!"

WILLIAM BARRET TRAVIS'S LAST HEROIC MESSAGE

R iding roughshod over Texas, the Mexican General Santa Anna trapped Colonel William Barret Travis and 200 brave Texans within the walls of the old Alamo Mission. Before they were slaughtered to a man, Commander Travis dispatched this letter, considered by many the most heroic document in American history. The battle cry "Remember the Alamo!" was to serve as Sam Houston's inspiration in his resounding victory and capture of Santa Anna at San Jacinto, which led to the establishment of Texas as an independent republic nearly a century and a half ago.

To the People of Texas & all Americans in the world—

Fby. 24th 1836—

Fellow citizens & compatriots—I am besieged, by a thousand or more of the Mexicans under Santa Anna—I have sustained a continual Bombardment & cannonade for 24 hours & have not lost a man—The enemy has demanded a surrender at discretion, otherwise the garrison are to be put to the <u>sword</u>, if the fort is taken—I have answered the demand with a cannon shot, & our flag still waves proudly from the walls—

I shall never surrender or retreat. Then, I call on you in the name of liberty, of patriotism & everything dear to the American character, to come to our aid, with all dispatch—The enemy is receiving reinforcements daily & will no doubt increase to three or four thousand in four or five days. If this call is neglected, I am determined to sustain myself as long as possible & die like a soldier who never forgets what is due to his own honor & that of his country—

> VICTORY OR DEATH
> William Barret Travis.
> Lt. Col. Comdt.

P.S. The Lord is on our side—When the enemy appeared in sight we had not three bushels of corn—We have since found in deserted houses 80 or 90 bushels & got into the walls 20 or 30 head of Beeves—

> Travis

Van Buren Opposes
the Welfare State

THE LESS GOVERNMENT INTERFERES,
THE BETTER

I n the great depression of 1837, Martin Van Buren refused to use his presidential powers to aid the ailing economy. In this message sent to members of Congress, the president explained why he deemed it his duty to take this unpopular stand.

Washington,
September 4, 1837

To the Congress of the United States:

All communities are apt to look to government for too much. Even in our own country, where its powers and duties are so strictly limited, we are prone to do so, especially at periods of sudden embarrassment and distress. But this ought not to be. The framers of our excellent Constitution and the people who approved it with calm and sagacious deliberation acted at the time on a sounder principle. They wisely judged that the less government interferes with private pursuits the better for the general prosperity. . . .

It is not its legitimate object to make men rich or to repair by direct grants of money . . . losses not incurred in the public service. . . . Its real duty—that duty the performance of which makes a good government the most precious of human blessings—is to enact and enforce a system of general laws . . . and to leave every citizen and every interest to reap under its benign protection the rewards of virtue, industry and prudence.

M. Van Buren

Jackson Declines a Tomb for a King

THE PLAIN CITIZENS ARE THE "SOVEREIGNS OF OUR GLORIOUS UNION"

A group of Andrew Jackson's admirers once proposed that a marble sarcophagus, containing the remains of a Roman emperor, be brought over from Palestine and used as Old Hickory's tomb. In the same democratic spirit that George Washington *refused a crown, the great champion of the common people declined the honor, stating that the plain republican citizens "are the sovereigns of our glorious union."*

March 27, 1845
Hermitage, Tenn.

Dear Sirs:

I must decline accepting the honor intended to be bestowed. I cannot consent that my mortal body shall be laid in a repository prepared for an Emperor or King.

My Republican feelings and principles forbid it; the simplicity of our system of government forbids it. Every monument erected to perpetuate the memory of our heroes and statesmen ought to bear evidence of the economy and simplicity of our Republican institutions and of the plainness of our Republican citizens, who are the sovereigns of our glorious union and whose virtue it is to perpetuate it. True virtue cannot exist where pomp and parade are the governing passions. It can only dwell with the people—the great laboring and producing classes—that form the bone and sinew of our Confederacy.

For these reasons I cannot accept the honor you and the president and directors of the National Institute intended to bestow. I cannot permit my remains to be the first in these United States to be deposited in a sarcophagus made for an Emperor or a King. I again repeat, please accept for yourself and convey to the president and directors of the National Institute, my most profound respects for the honor you and they intended to bestow. I have prepared an humble depository for my mortal body besides that wherein lies my beloved wife, where without any pomp or parade, I have requested, when my God calls me to sleep with my fathers, to be laid; for both of us there to remain until the last trumpet sounds to call the dead to judgment, when we, I hope, shall rise together, clothed with the heavenly body promised to all who believe in our glorious Redeemer who died for us that we might live, and by whose atonement I hope for a blessed immortality.

I am, with great respect, your friend and fellow citizen,

Andrew Jackson

THE AUTHOR OF
"HOME SWEET HOME"

~~~

NEVER HAD A HOME OF HIS OWN

J ust one year after he wrote this letter, John Howard Payne died at Tunis, far from the homeland he was representing as American consul. Payne considered it strange that the author of the popular song "Home Sweet Home" never had a home of his own and never expected to have one. Ironic though it seems, it perhaps explains his heartfelt feeling that there is no place like home.

Washington, March 3, 1851

Hon. C.E. Clarke.
My Dear Sir:

It affords me great pleasure to comply with your request for the words of "Home Sweet Home". Surely there is something strange in the fact that it should have been my lot to cause so many people in the world to boast of the delights of home, when I never had a home of my own, and never expect to have one, now— especially since those here at Washington who possess the power seem so reluctant to allow me the means of earning one! In the hope that I may again and often have the gratification of meeting you, believe me, my dear sir,

Yours, most faithfully,
John Howard Payne

Thoreau Has a Library of 900 Books

~

MORE THAN 700 HE WROTE HIMSELF

*L*ike many of our best writers, Henry D. Thoreau, author of the famous Walden, was unable to find a publisher for his A Week on the Concord and Merrimack Rivers. At his own expense he had a bookseller print 1,000 copies. After many months, the dealer returned to Thoreau 706 books still unsold. The great naturalist told in his journal manuscript why his collection of books was then unique among libraries.

Sunday
Oct. 30, 1853

For a year or two past, my publisher, falsely so called, has been writing from time to time to ask what disposition should be made of the copies of A Week on the Concord and Merrimack Rivers still on hand, and at last suggesting that he had use for the room they occupied in his cellar. So I had them all sent to me here, and they have arrived to-day by express, filling the man's wagon—706 copies out of an edition of 1000 which I bought of Munroe four years ago and have been ever since paying for, and have not quite paid for yet. The wares are sent to me at last, and I have an opportunity to examine my purchase. They are something more substantial than fame, as my back knows, which has borne them up two flights of stairs to a place similar to that to which they trace their origin. Of the remaining two hundred and ninety and odd, seventy-five were given away, the rest sold. I have now a library of nearly nine hundred volumes, over seven hundred of which I wrote myself. Is it not well that the author should behold the fruits of his labor? My works are piled up on one side of my chamber half as high as my head, my opera omnia. This is authorship; these are the work of my brain. . . .

Henry D. Thoreau

A Celebrated Young Lady
OVERCOMES SEX DISCRIMINATION

L ong before the days of the Equal Rights Amendment, a young woman received a pink slip of dismissal from the U.S. Patent Office. She wrote the commissioner of patents, asking him to intercede with the secretary of the interior on her behalf. The commissioner complied and received this curt reply. The "lady in question" was Clara Barton who, after her dismissal, founded the American Red Cross.

[1854]

Dear Commissioner:

There is every disposition on my part to do anything for the lady in question except to retain her or any of the other females who work in the Patent Office. I have no objection to the employment of females in duties they are competent to discharge, but there is such obvious impropriety in the mixing of the sexes within the walls of public office that I have determined to arrest the practice.

Robert McClelland
Secretary of the Interior

ROBERT E. LEE CONDEMNS CIVIL WAR
SAVE IN DEFENSE OF HIS NATIVE STATE, HE WILL DRAW HIS SWORD NO MORE

S tationed at a frontier post near San Antonio in January 1861, before the outbreak of the Civil War, Robert E. Lee wrote to one of his sons "that he could anticipate no greater calamity than a dissolution of the Union." Torn between his devotion to his country and his duty to his native state, he returned to "share the miseries" of his people in Virginia. Years later, when Dwight Eisenhower was criticized for having a picture of Lee in his White House office, he defended the Confederate commander-in-chief as one of the greatest Americans.

[Dear Son,]

Secession is nothing but revolution. The framers of our Constitution never exhausted so much labour, wisdom and forbearance in its formation, and surrounded it with so many guards and securites, if it was intended to be broken by any member of the Confederacy at will. . . . In 1808, when the New England States resisted Mr. Jefferson's Embargo law, and [when] the Hartford Convention assembled, secession was termed treason by Virginian statesmen; what can it be now? Still, a Union that can only be maintained by swords and bayonets, and in which strife and civil war are to take the place of brotherly love and kindness, has no charm for me. If the Union is dissolved, the government disrupted, I shall return to my native state and share the miseries of my people. Save in her defense, I will draw my sword no more.

R. E. Lee

PIERCE CALLS FOR A MEETING OF FIVE PRESIDENTS
TO SEE HOW THE CIVIL WAR MIGHT BE AVERTED

Four days after the attack on Fort Sumter, ex-president Franklin Pierce wrote to ex-president Martin Van Buren, suggesting that he call a meeting of the five living ex-presidents to consider how the Civil War might be averted.

Ex-presidents seem to have trouble agreeing even on such vital issues as war and peace. Only four times in this century have as many as four presidents been living at one time. But like the five presidents in 1861, only once in this century did four presidents meet. In October 1981, Richard Nixon, Gerald Ford, and Jimmy Carter posed for photographs with Ronald Reagan before the three ex-presidents flew to Anwar Sadat's funeral.

Concord, N.H., April 16, 1861

My Dear Sir,

The present unparalleled crisis in the affairs of our country is, I have no doubt, filling you, as it is me, with the profoundest sorrow. Is there any human power which can avert the conflict of arms now apparently near at hand between the two sections of the Union? . . .

If the five retired Presidents of the United States, still living, were to meet at the earliest practicable day at the city where the Constitution was formed, might not their consultation, if it should result in concurrence of judgment, reach the Administration and the country with some degree of power? No man can with propriety summon such a meeting but yourself. I feel that we ought not to omit at least an effort. Whatever the result may be, can we permit our remaining days or years to be disturbed by the consciousness that, after having been honored by the confidence of the Republic, we have passively seen it drift to destruction.

Should this suggestion commend itself to your judgment, will you communicate with Mr. Tyler, Mr. Fillmore and Mr. Buchanan, and advise me of the result.

Respectfully & truly, your friend,

Franklin Pierce

Alexander Hamilton's last letter to his wife, Eliza, before his fatal duel with Aaron Burr. (page 40)

Passy, Mar. 18. 1785.

My dear Friend,

    My Nephew, Mr. Williams, will have the honour of delivering you this Line. It is to request from you a List of a few good Books to the Value of about Twenty five Pounds, such as are most proper to inculcate Principles of sound Religion & just Government. A New Town in the State of Massachusetts, having done me the honour of naming itself after me, and proposing to build a Steeple to their meeting House if I would give them a Bell, I have advis'd the sparing themselves the Expence of a Steeple at present, and that they would accept of Books instead of a Bell, Sense being preferable to Sound. These are therefore intended as the commencement of a little Parochial Library, for the Use of a Society of intelligent respectable Farmers, such as our Country People generally consist of. Besides your own Works I would only mention, on the Recommendation

of

"Sense being preferable to Sound," Benjamin Franklin sent books instead of a bell to a town named in his honor. (page 33)

of my Sister, Stennett's Discourses on personal Religion,
which may be one Book of the Number, if you know
it and approve of it. With the highest Esteem &
Respect, I am ever, my dear Friend,

Yours most affectionately
(Signed)   B. Franklin

Concord N.H. April 16. 1861

My Dear Sir,

The present unparalleled crisis in the affairs of our country, is I have no doubt filling you, as it is me with the profoundest sorrow. Is there any human power which can avert the conflict of arms now apparently near at hand, between the two sections of the Union? The news to night would seem to indicate that the Central and Border States (at least Virginia, Kentucky and Tennessee) will in view of the military movements of the North, cast their lot with the states already seceded.

There is no time for effective assemblages of the people — No time for conventions or protracted discussion — But it has occurred to me that you may take measures to suspend active military operations, secure opportunity for reflection in the face of present dangers, and save the most fearful calamity which has ever impended over a nation.

Franklin Pierce's letter to Martin Van Buren suggesting that a meeting of five living ex-presidents might help avert the Civil War. (page 63)

If the five retired Presidents of the United States, still living, were to meet at the earliest practicable day at the city where the Constitution was formed, might not their consultation, if it should result in concurrence of judgment reach the Administration and the Country with some degree of ~~authority~~ power? No man can with propriety summon such a meeting but yourself. I feel that we ought not to omit, at least an effort. Whatever the result may be, can we permit our remaining days or years to be disturbed by the consciousness that, after having been honored by the confidence of the Republic we have passively seen it drift to destruction.

Should this suggestion commend itself to your judgment will you communicate with Mr Tyler, Mr Filmore and Mr Buchanan and advise me of the result.

Respectfully & Truly
Your friend
Franklin Pierce

Ex President
Martin Van Buren
Kinderhook. N.Y.

Executive Mansion,

Washington, July 14   , 1863.

Major General Meade

I have just seen your despatch to Gen. Halleck, asking to be relieved of your command, because of a supposed censure of mine. I am very — very — grateful to you for the magnificient success you gave the cause of the country at Gettysburg; and I am sorry now to be the author of the slightest pain to you. But I was in such deep distress myself that I could not restrain some expression of it. I have been oppressed nearly ever since the battles at Gettysburg, by what appeared to be evidences that yourself, and Gen. Couch, and Gen. Smith, were not seeking a collision with the enemy, but were trying to get him across the river without another battle. What these evidences were, if you please, I hope to tell you at some time, when we shall both feel better. The case, summarily stated is this. You fought and beat the enemy at Gettysburg; and, of course, to say the least, his loss was as great as yours. He retreated; and you did not, as it seemed to me, pressingly pursue him; but a flood in the river detained him, till, by slow degrees, you were again upon him. You had at least twenty thous-

24806

Abraham Lincoln's reproachful letter to General Meade was never sent. (page 66)

and veteran troops directly with you, and as many more raw ones within supporting distance, all in addition to those who fought with you, at Gettysburg; while it was not possible that he had received a single recruit; and yet you stood, and let the floods run down, bridges be built, and the enemy move away at his leisure, without attacking him. And Couch and Smith! The latter left Carlisle in time, upon all ordinary calculation, to have aided you in the last battle at Gettysburg; but he did not arrive. At the end of more than ten days, I believe twelve, under constant urging, he reached Hagerstown from Carlisle, which is not an inch over fifty-five miles, if so much. And Couch's movement was very little different—

Again, my dear general, I do not believe you appreciate the magnitude of the misfortune involved in Lee's escape— He was within your easy grasp, and to have closed upon him would, in connection with the our other late successes, have ended the war— As it is, the war will be prolonged indefinitely. If you could not safely attack Lee last Monday, how can you possibly do so South of the river, when you can take with you very few more than two thirds of the force you then had in hand? It would be unreasonable to expect, and I do not expect you can now effect much. Your golden opportunity is gone, and I am distressed immeasurably because of it.

I beg you will not consider this a prosecution, or persecution of yourself. As you had learned that I was dissatisfied, I have thought it best to kindly tell you why.

24807

LINCOLN'S CLASSIC CONSOLATION LETTER

AFTER THE DEATH OF COLONEL ELLSWORTH

Less famous than Abraham Lincoln's letter to Mrs. Bixby, "the mother of five sons who have died gloriously on the field of battle,"* but a more moving classic of consolation, was the president's letter to the parents of twenty-four-year-old Colonel Ellsworth. Considered the first casualty of the Civil War, he was fatally shot by the owner of a hotel in Alexandria, which was displaying a Confederate flag that Ellsworth was climbing up to remove.

Ellsworth had served as a law clerk in Lincoln's law office and accompanied the president's party on the train to Washington. Lincoln offered him a high post in the War Department, but Ellsworth preferred active duty as commander of a Zouave† regiment. His tragic death was a personal loss to Abraham Lincoln as well as to his country.

Washington D.C.
May 25. 1861

To the Father and Mother of Col.
Elmer E. Ellsworth:

My dear Sir and Madam,

In the untimely loss of your noble son, our affliction here, is scarcely less than your own. So much of promised usefulness to one's country, and of bright hopes for one's self and friends, have rarely been so suddenly dashed, as in his fall. In size, in years, and in youthful appearance, a boy only, his power to command men, was surpassingly great. This power, combined with a fine

---

*Lincoln was misinformed as to the number of sons Mrs. Bixby lost in the war. Two sons, not five, were killed; two sons were reported to have deserted and one to have been honorably discharged.

†Several volunteer Union regiments adopted the colorful oriental uniforms of the Algerian-French infantry.

intellect, an indomitable energy, and a taste altogether military, constituted in him, as seemed to me, the best natural talent, in that department, I ever knew. And yet he was singularly modest and deferential in social intercourse. My acquaintance with him began less than two years ago; yet through the latter half of the intervening period, it was as intimate as the disparity of our ages, and my engrossing engagements, would permit. To me, he appeared to have no indulgences or pastimes; and I never heard him utter a profane, or an intemperate word. What was conclusive of his good heart, he never forgot his parents. The honors he labored for so laudably, and, in the sad end, so gallantly gave his life, he meant for them, no less than for himself.

In the hope that it may be no intrusion upon the sacredness of your sorrow, I have ventured to address you this tribute to the memory of my young friend, and your brave and early fallen child.

May God give you the consolation which is beyond all earthly power. Sincerely your friend in a common affliction—

A. Lincoln

JULY 4TH VICTORIES AT VICKSBURG AND GETTYSBURG

⌒∽⌒

THE LETTER LINCOLN WROTE BUT DID NOT SEND

O*nce again July fourth proved to be of mystic significance in the history of the country. For on that same day, in 1863, the defenders of Vicksburg surrendered to Ulysses S. Grant, and Robert E. Lee's forces were defeated at Gettysburg. Retreating to the bank of the Potomac, high waters prevented the Confederates from crossing—but General George Meade did not attack Lee's cornered army. Overcome with grief because Meade did not pursue his advantage and end the war, Abraham Lincoln wrote this reproachful letter but never sent it, knowing the loss to be irreparable.*

Executive Mansion,
Washington, D.C.,
July 14, 1863.

Major General Meade:

I have just seen your despatch to General Halleck, asking to be relieved of your command because of a supposed censure of mine. I am very, very grateful to you for the magnificient success you gave the cause of the country at Gettysburg; and I am sorry now to be the author of the slightest pain to you. But I was in such deep distress myself that I could not restrain some expression of it. I have been oppressed nearly ever since the battles at Gettysburg by what appeared to be evidences that yourself and Gen. Couch and Gen. Smith were not seeking a collision with the enemy, but were trying to get him across the river without another battle. What these evidences were, if you please, I hope to tell you at some time when we shall both feel better. The case, summarily stated, is this: You fought and beat the enemy at Gettysburg and, of course, to say the least, his loss was as great as yours. He retreated, and you did not, as it seemed to me, pressingly pursue him; but a flood in the river detained him till, by slow degrees, you were again upon him. You had at least twenty thousand veteran troops directly with you, and as many more raw ones within supporting distance, all in addition to those who fought with you at Gettysburg, while it was not possible that he had received a single recruit, and yet you stood and let the flood run down, bridges be built, and the enemy move away at his leisure without attacking him. And Couch and Smith! The latter left Carlisle in time, upon all ordinary calculation, to have aided you in the last battle at Gettysburg, but he did not arrive. At the end of more than ten days, I believe twelve, under constant urging, he reached Hagerstown from Carlisle, which is not an inch over fifty-five miles, if so much, and Couch's movement was very little different.

Again, my dear general, I do not believe you appreciate the magnitude of the misfortune involved in Lee's escape. He was within your easy grasp, and to have closed upon him would, in connection with our other late successes, have ended the war. As it is, the war will be prolonged indefinitely. If you could not safely attack Lee last Monday, how can you possibly do so south of the river, when you can take with you very few more than two-thirds of the force you then had in hand?

It would be unreasonable to expect, and I do not expect [that] you can now effect much. Your golden opportunity is gone, and I am distressed immeasurably because of it.

I beg you will not consider this a prosecution or persecution of yourself. As you had learned that I was dissatisfied, I have thought it best to kindly tell you why.

A. Lincoln

THE LONG AND THE SHORT OF IT AT GETTYSBURG

THE SPEECHES OF EDWARD EVERETT AND ABRAHAM LINCOLN

E dward Everett, the distinguished orator and educator, was invited to deliver the main address in 1863 at the dedication of the national cemetery at Gettysburg. Abraham Lincoln was asked to say only a few brief words. He jotted down some notes on the train on his way to Gettysburg and then wrote his few words, in his hotel room, on the morning of the ceremony.

The newspapers the next day were full of praise for Everett's two-hour oration. Many disparagingly commented that "Lincoln also spoke." Everett was one of the first to recognize the immortality in Lincoln's words. He wrote magnanimously to the president: "I should be glad if I could flatter myself that I came as near the central idea of the occasion in two hours as you did in two minutes."

With characteristic humility Lincoln replied: "You could not have been excused to make a short address, nor I a long one." This epigrammatic exchange, between two great minds of their time, deserves an honored place with Lincoln's most famous speech.

Edward Everett to Abraham Lincoln

Dear President Lincoln:

I beg leave in this way to thank you for your great thoughtfulness for my daughter's accommodation on the platform yesterday. . . . Permit me also to express my great admiration of the thoughts expressed by you . . . at the consecration of the cemetery. I should be glad if I could flatter myself that I came as near to the central idea of the occasion in two hours as you did in two minutes. My son, who parted from me at Baltimore, and my daughter concur in this sentiment.

Your obedient servant,
Edward Everett

Abraham Lincoln to Edward Everett

Washington, D.C.
November 20, 1863

My dear Sir:

Your kind note of to-day is received. In our respective parts yesterday, you could not have been excused to make a short address, nor I a long one. I am pleased to know that, in your judgment, the little I did say was not entirely a failure.

Of course I knew Mr. Everett would not fail, and yet, while the whole discourse was eminently satisfactory, and will be of great value, there were passages in it which transcended my expectations.

The point made against the theory of the General Government being only an agency whose principals are the States, was new to me, and, as I think is one of the best arguments for the national supremacy. The tribute to our noble women for their angel ministering to the suffering soldiers surpasses in its way, as do the subjects of it, whatever has gone before.

Your obedient servant,
A. Lincoln

CHARLES W. ELIOT ON LINCOLN'S ASSASSINATION

⚜

IT "STAINED INDELIBLY THE ANNALS OF THE REPUBLIC"

*I*n Rome, where he had gone for special studies at age thirty, *Charles W. Eliot received the news of Lincoln's assassination. The great educator, who later became the president of Harvard for forty distinguished years, wrote his mother of what a terrible shock it was and philosophized on its tragic effect on the country. Eliot was clairvoyant when he wrote that "our struggle is a struggle of humanity against barbarism," because the struggle still goes on today.*

Dear Mother—

Thursday, Apr. 27, in the morning we got the news of the assassination at Washington, the bare facts without particulars, Seward's recovery being said to be hopeless. It must have come just as suddenly to you at home. What a horrible shock it was— the loss of great battles would have been as nothing—battles and campaigns can be retrieved, but now the horrible crime of assassination for political reasons has stained indelibly the annals of the republic.

That is the horror of it to my mind—the men can be replaced, the policy of the government will probably be unchanged, the war will go on without any intermission of faltering, but the dreadful fact remains that an American President has been assassinated by an American. This is a crowning fruit of slavery to our eyes, but to the world and history it is a legitimate fruit of American institutions, such as they have actually been since the Republic was founded. First, civil war, and now, political assassination. Oh, are we copying Rome?

We have been proud of the security of our public servants without guards or any sort of protection against the people—we have said that assassination might be a possible crime for French or Italian or Mexican republicans, but never for Americans.

. . . In our admiration of the soldierly virtues of Lee and his army, we felt like embracing our enemies and welcoming them back to Peace and Country. But here is the most dastardly crime thrown across the path of conciliation. It is the last proof that our struggle is a struggle of humanity against barbarism, but how shall we redeem or get rid of the barbarians?

I am no worshipper of men—even now, I don't like to hear Lincoln's name put too near Washington's, but his character seems to me a rough and ungraceful but truly noble growth of republican institutions. He grew to his work, which was holy and it hallowed him. You can count on your fingers the names which History will rank with his. It is the glory and strength of our institutions that we do not depend on any one man or any men for security or for the working vigor of our government. If the assassins thought that the government would be thrown into confusion by their work, they will be disappointed—Lincoln's death will consecrate his policy in the eyes of the people and men will be found to carry it out. He did not lead the people—he rather followed the wisest and best thought of the people, and his successors will do likewise. . . .

Charles W. Eliot

THE REAL WILLIAM TECUMSEH SHERMAN
"WOULD NOT SUBJUGATE THE SOUTH"

T hey call me a barbarian, vandal, a monster," wrote William Tecumseh Sherman. The South regarded him as one of the cruelest, most relentless generals. Yet when we read this confidential letter to one of his Southern friends, we see that Sherman really meant it when he said, "War is Hell."

Mrs. Annie Gilman Bower,
Baltimore, Maryland.

Your welcome letter of June 18th came to me amid the sound of
battle, and as you say, little did I dream when I knew you, playing
as a schoolgirl on Sullivan's Island beach, that I should control a
vast army pointing, like the swarm of Alaric, toward the plains of
the South.

Why, oh, why, is this? If I know my own heart, it beats as
warmly as ever toward those kind and generous families that
greeted us with such warm hospitality in days long past . . . and
today . . . were any and all cherished circle . . . to come to me as
of old, the stern feelings of duty would melt as snow before a
genial sun, and I believe I would strip my own children that they
might be sheltered.

And yet they call me a barbarian, vandal, a monster. . . . All I
pretend to say, on earth as in heaven, man must submit to some
arbiter. . . . I would not subjugate the South . . . but I would
make every citizen of the land obey the common law, submit to
the same that we do—no more, no less—our equals and not our
superiors. . . . God only knows how reluctantly we accepted the
issue, but once the issue joined, like in other ages, the Northern
races, though slow to anger, once aroused are more terrible than
the more inflammable of the South. Even yet my heart bleeds
when I say that instead of appealing to war they should have
appealed to reason, to our Congress, to our courts, to religion,
and to the experience of history, then will I say, peace,
peace. . . . Whether I shall live to see this period is problematical,
but you may and may tell your mother and sisters that I never
forgot one kind look or greeting, or ever wished to efface its
remembrance, but putting on the armor of war I did it that our
common country should not perish in infamy and disgrace. . . . I
hope when the clouds of anger and passion are dispersed, and
truth emerges bright and clear, you and all who knew me in early
years will not blush that we were once close friends. . . .

W. T. Sherman

THE MIND OF AN ASSASSIN

<the ornament>

A LETTER OF CHARLES GUITEAU, WHO FATALLY SHOT PRESIDENT GARFIELD

In July 1881, President James A. Garfield was shot in the Washington railroad station by Charles Guiteau. After the shooting and his arrest, this letter was found in his possession. Apparently the assassin did not know that the president survived two and a half more months. Garfield had been besieged by office seekers, many of whom like Guiteau were unsuccessful. Although a failure at every undertaking, he wanted to be ambassador to Austria or consul general in Paris. Ignored by Garfield, Guiteau believed that he had been appointed by the Almighty to do away with the president to "save the Republic." While motives differ, this letter of Guiteau gives an insight into the distorted mind of one assassin.

Washington July 2nd
1881

To the White House

The President's tragic death was a sad necessity, but it will unite the Republican party and save the Republic. Life is a flimsy dream and it matters little when one goes. A human life is of small value. During the war thousands of brave boys went down without a fear.

I presume the President was a Christian and that he will be happier in Paradise than here.

It will be no worse for Mrs. Garfield, dear soul, to part with her husband this way, than by natural death. He is liable to go at any time, anyway.

I had no ill will toward the President. His death was a political necessity.

I am a lawyer, theologian, and politician. I am a stalwart of the Stalwarts.

I was with General Grant and the rest of our men in New York during the canvass.

73

I have some papers for the Press which I shall leave with Byron Andrews, and his co-journalists, at 1420 N.Y. ave. where all the reporters can see them.

I am going to the jail.

Charles Guiteau

PRESIDENT ARTHUR ORDERS A SALUTE OF THE BRITISH FLAG

ON THE HUNDREDTH ANNIVERSARY OF THE BATTLE OF YORKTOWN

B ritish General Cornwallis's surrender in Yorktown in 1781 marked the virtual end of the American Revolution, although the Treaty of Paris was not signed until a year and a half later. On the hundredth anniversary of Yorktown, President Chester A. Arthur ordered the salute of the British flag, symbolizing the healing of wounds and the restoration of friendly relations between the United States and Great Britain.

A century later, President Ronald Reagan and President François Mitterrand of France met at Yorktown to celebrate the two-hundredth anniversary of the victory of American troops with the help of the French navy.

Yorktown, Va.,
October 19, 1881

Executive Order:

In recognition of the friendly relations so long and so happily subsisting between Great Britain and the United States, in the trust and confidence of peace and good will between the two countries for all the centuries to come, and especially as a mark of the profound respect entertained by the American people for the illustrious sovereign and gracious lady who sits upon the British throne.

It is hereby ordered, that at the close of the ceremonies commemorative of the valor and success of our forefathers in their patriotic struggle for independence the British flag shall be saluted by the forces of the Army and Navy of the United States now at Yorktown.

The Secretary of War and the Secretary of the Navy will give orders accordingly.

C. Arthur

MARK TWAIN TO WALT WHITMAN ON HIS SEVENTIETH BIRTHDAY

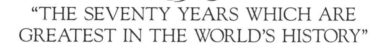

"THE SEVENTY YEARS WHICH ARE GREATEST IN THE WORLD'S HISTORY"

On July 4, 1855, Walt Whitman published, at his own expense, the volume of poems Leaves of Grass. It was severely criticized for its glorification of sex until Ralph Waldo Emerson praised it as a classic. During the Civil War, between writing poetry, Whitman served the Union cause by nursing wounded Union soldiers returned from the front. On his seventieth birthday, Mark Twain was inspired to send the poet of democracy this letter, which critic Lewis Mumford considered one of the classic letters of all time.

May 31, 1889

To Walt Whitman:

You have lived just the seventy years which are greatest in the world's history and richest in benefit and advancement to its peoples. These seventy years have done more to widen the interval between man and the other animals than was accomplished by any of the five centuries which preceded them.

What great births you have witnessed! The steam press, the steamship, the steelship, the railroad, the perfect cotton gin, the telegraph, the phonograph, photogravure, the electrotype, the gaslight, the electric light, the sewing machine and the amazing infinitely varied and innumerable products of coal tar, those latest and strangest marvels of a marvelous age. And you have seen even greater births than these; for you have seen the application of anesthesia to surgery-practice, whereby the ancient dominion of pain, which began with the first created life, came to an end on this earth forever, you have seen the slave set free, you have seen monarchy banished from France and reduced in England to a machine which makes an imposing show of diligence and attention to business, but isn't connected with the works. Yes you have indeed seen much—but tarry for a while, for the greatest is yet to come. Wait thirty years, and then look out over the earth! You shall see marvels upon marvels added to those whose nativity you have witnessed; and conspicuous above them you shall see their formidable Result—man at almost his full stature at last!—and still growing, visibly growing while you look. . . . Wait till you see that great figure appear, and catch the far glint of the sun upon his banner; then you may depart satisfied, as knowing you have seen him for whom the earth was made, and that he will proclaim that human wheat is more than human tares, and proceed to organize human values on that basis.

Mark Twain

TEDDY ROOSEVELT REFUSES NOBEL PRIZE MONEY

"LIKE BEING GIVEN MONEY FOR RESCUING A MAN FROM DROWNING"

Theodore Roosevelt, ever ready with the "big stick," assumed the role of mediator in arranging the peace conference at Portsmouth, New Hampshire, in 1906 which ended the Russo-Japanese War. For this triumph of diplomacy he was awarded the Nobel prize. In a remarkable letter to his son Kermit, President Roosevelt explained why he could not accept the prize money. He eventually gave the money for the benefit of American soldiers in World War I—a strange employment of funds for peace.

December 5, 1906

Dear Kermit:

I have been a little puzzled over the Nobel prize. It appears that there is a large sum of money—they say about $40,000.00—that goes with it. Now, I hate to do anything foolish . . . But Mother and I talked it over and came to the conclusion that . . . I could not accept money given to me for making peace between two nations, especially when I was able to make peace simply because I was President.

To receive money for making peace would in any event be a little too much like being given money for rescuing a man from drowning. . . . Altogether Mother and I felt that there was no alternative and that I would have to apply the money to some public purpose. But I hated to have to come to the decision, because I very much wisht for the extra money to leave all you children. . . .

Your loving father,
Theodore Roosevelt

WOODROW WILSON OFFERS TO RESIGN

❦

IF DEFEATED FOR A SECOND TERM

W hen his election to a second term was in doubt, President Woodrow Wilson proposed a unique plan for his successor to assume immediate power. In Wilson's time, the newly elected president was not inaugurated until March, instead of January, and the secretary of state, not the speaker of the House, was next in line of succession. Wilson won a second term, so his resignation was not required.

November 5, 1916

Secretary of State Robert Lansing

Dear Mr. Lansing,

What would it be my duty to do were Mr. [Charles Evans] Hughes to be elected? Four months would elapse before he could take charge of the affairs of the government, and during those four months I would be without such moral backing from the nation as would be necessary to steady and control our relations with other governments. I would be known to be the rejected, not the accredited, spokesman of the country; and yet the accredited spokesman would be without legal authority to speak for the nation. Such a situation would be fraught with the gravest dangers. The direction of the foreign policy of the government would in effect have been taken out of my hands and yet its new definition would be impossible until March.

I feel that it would be my duty to relieve the country of the perils of such a situation at once. The course I have in mind is dependent upon the consent and cooperation of the Vice President; but if I could gain his consent of the plan, I would ask your permission to invite Mr. Hughes to become Secretary of State and would then join the Vice President in resigning, and thus open to Mr. Hughes the immediate succession to the Presidency.

Woodrow Wilson

THE ZIMMERMANN TELEGRAM

PROPOSES A GERMAN-MEXICAN ALLIANCE

Second only to the sinking of the Lusitania *in its importance in fanning the flame of anti-German feeling in the United States was the publication in March 1917 of this secret dispatch from the German foreign minister, Arthur Zimmermann, to his minister in Mexico. Its release by President Woodrow Wilson strengthened those who advocated American entry into World War I.*

Berlin, Jan. 19, 1917.

On the 1st of February we intend to begin submarine warfare unrestricted. In spite of this, it is our intention to endeavor to keep neutral the United States of America.

If this attempt is not successful, we propose an alliance on the following basis with Mexico: That we shall make war together and together make peace. We shall give general financial support, and it is understood that Mexico is to reconquer the lost territory in New Mexico, Texas, and Arizona. The details are left to you for settlement.

You are instructed to inform the President of Mexico of the above in the greatest confidence as soon as it is certain that there will be an outbreak of war with the United States, and suggest that the President of Mexico, on his own initiative should communicate with Japan suggesting adherence at once to his plan. At the same time, offer to mediate between Germany and Japan.

Please call to the attention of the President of Mexico that the employment of ruthless submarine warfare now promises to compel England to make peace in a few months.

Zimmermann

"THE FIRST WOMAN PRESIDENT"

EDITH GALT WILSON ACTS AS SURROGATE FOR HER HELPLESS HUSBAND

Worn out by his futile fight to win a lasting peace after World War I, President Woodrow Wilson suffered a complete physical collapse in the midst of his second term.

Edith Galt Wilson has often been called the first woman president because she made all of the important decisions for her desperately ill husband. While Wilson lay paralyzed, she guided his hand in signing important official documents.

The Wilsons were ideally devoted to each other. Wilson had once sent Mrs. Galt (later Mrs. Wilson) a corsage with a card which read, "You are the only woman I know who can wear an orchid. Generally it is the orchid that wears the woman." Years later, Edith Galt Wilson was moved to send the helpless president this short but eloquent expression of her affection.

Dearest:

I will stand by you—not for duty, not for pity, not for honour—but for love—trusting, protecting comprehending love. . . .

I am so tired I could put my head down on the desk and go to sleep—but nothing could bring me real rest until I had pledged to you my love and my allegiance.

Your own
Edith

THOMAS EDISON WOULD NEED NO SLEEP

~~~

IF THE SUN WOULD SHINE TWENTY-FOUR HOURS A DAY

*T*homas Edison once confirmed the astounding story that he decided to invent the electric light, after the gas company cut off his supply, when he was behind in paying his bills.

Some sixty years ago, when there was no shortage of energy, business writer William Feather asked Thomas Edison if it was true that he and his assistants worked with a minimum of sleep. Edison replied that it was true and explained why electric lights made it possible.

From the Laboratory of Thomas A. Edison
Orange, N.J.

September 16, 1919

Dear Mr. Feather:

I received your letter of September 10 in regard to sleep. Until the last six years, and over a period of 40 years, I and my experimental assistants worked on an average 18 hours daily. New men found it very difficult to get used to 4 or 5 hours sleep, but in a short time they became accustomed to it and I have never heard of any one of them being injured.

I find that men who once worked with me for a number of years and then left, kept up the habit of working long hours. I think any person can get used to it. One remarkable thing that they all agree on is that it stops dreaming. This is perhaps due to a deeper sleep.

If the world had been differently arranged and the sun had shone continuously, I do not think that anybody would require or take sleep. There seems to be no actual reason why we should sleep, from a scientific standpoint.

I noticed in automobiling through Switzerland that the towns which had electric lights had many new buildings and the people were active and on the streets at 12:00 o'clock, midnight, whereas in towns without electric lights, everybody was in bed about 8:30 and the town was a dead one.

Thomas A. Edison

RUSSIA PLEDGES ETERNAL FRIENDSHIP TO THE UNITED STATES

AND THANKS HERBERT HOOVER FOR SAVING MILLIONS OF STARVING RUSSIANS

ollowing World War I, the successor to Lenin expressed Russia's heartfelt gratitude to Herbert Hoover and his American Relief Administration for saving millions of Russians from death and entire districts from catastrophe. On behalf of the Peoples Commissars, its acting president assured Hoover that the USSR would never forget the help given them and pledged future friendship with America—a pledge that Russia has long since failed to remember.

Moscow, Kremlin
July 10, 1923

Herbert C. Hoover, Director
The American Relief Administration

In the trying hour of a great and overwhelming disaster, the people of the United States, represented by the A.R.A., responded to the needs of the population, already exhausted by intervention and blockade, in the famine stricken parts of Russia and Federated Republics.

Unselfishly, the A.R.A. came to the aid of the people and

organized on a broad scale the supply and distribution of food products and other articles of prime necessity.

Due to the enormous and entirely disinterested efforts of the A.R.A., millions of people of all ages were saved from death, and entire districts and even cities were saved from the horrible catastrophe which threatened them.

Now when the famine is over and the colossal work of the A.R.A. comes to a close, the Soviet of Peoples Commissars, in the name of the millions of people saved and in the name of all the working people of Soviet Russia and the Federated Republics counts it a duty to express before the whole world its deepest thanks to this organization, to its leader, Herbert Hoover, to its representative in Russia, Colonel Haskell, and to all its workers, and to declare that the people inhabiting the Union of Soviet Socialist Republics will never forget the help given them by the American people, through the A.R.A., seeing in it a pledge of the future friendship of the two nations.

L. Kamenev,
Acting President of the
Council of Peoples
Commisars

BERNARD BARUCH PREDICTS THE 1929 CRASH

FINANCIAL PROBLEMS DATE TO 1927

S everal months before it happened in 1929, Bernard Baruch gave his reason for predicting a great stock market crash to Senator William H. King of Utah. He dated the beginnings of the problem to actions taken by the Federal Reserve System in 1927. The argument is remarkably similar to ones we are still hearing today about the Federal Reserve and the effects of its policies on the economy.

Dear Senator King:

The original difficulty started in 1927 when the Federal Reserve System reduced its rate to 3½% either for the purpose of forcing gold out or stimulating our exports. Whether that was wise or not, they evidently had in mind the accomplishment of some definite, constructive purpose. But they overlooked the fact that when they artificially reduced the rate . . . there would be a re-evaluation of securities and an artificial stimulus to business. Whatever their purpose was, they should have acted very promptly in raising the rate and that would have stopped the things they are now objecting to and which they directly caused.

Bernard Baruch

HERBERT HOOVER ACCEPTS THE PRESIDENTIAL NOMINATION

SAYING HE IS INDEBTED TO HIS COUNTRY

The Republican National Convention of 1928 chose Herbert Hoover as its candidate for president, in recognition of the great services he had performed for his country. When notified of his selection, Hoover accepted the nomination but not the tribute, saying, "My country owes me no debt."

Washington, D.C.
June 14, 1928

George H. Moses
Chairman Republican National Convention
Kansas City, Missouri

You convey too great a compliment when you say that I have earned the right to the presidential nomination. No man can establish such an obligation upon any part of the American people. My country owes me no debt. It gave me schooling, independence of action, opportunity for service and honor. In no other land could a boy from a country village, without inheritance or influential friends, look forward with unbounded hope.

My whole life has taught me what America means. I am indebted to my country beyond any human power to repay. . . . It has called me into the cabinets of two Presidents. By these experiences I have observed the burdens and responsibilities of the greatest office in the world. That office touches the happiness of every home. It deals with the peace of nations. No man could think of it except in terms of solemn consecration.

Herbert Hoover

PIONEER AVIATRIX AMELIA EARHART
HAS A PREMONITION OF A TRAGIC END

*A*lthough her parents disapproved, Amelia Earhart took up flying and became one of the outstanding pioneers in aviation. She became the first woman to fly solo across the Atlantic, from Newfoundland to Ireland.

In 1937 she attempted to fly around the world with Lt. Commander Fred Noonan in a twin-engine Lockheed. Two-thirds of the way, the plane suddenly disappeared near Howland Island in the Pacific Ocean.

After Amelia's mother was notified, she found this note written in anticipation of the tragic ending.

Mother:

Even though I have lost, the adventure was worthwhile. Our family tends to be too secure. My life has really been very happy and I didn't mind contemplating its end in the midst of it.

Amelia

WHY EINSTEIN PERSUADED ROOSEVELT TO MAKE THE ATOM BOMB

"FRIGHTFUL TO IMAGINE" IF HITLER POSSESSED THIS WEAPON

J ohn Napier was a Scottish mathematician who died in 1617. He is said to have invented a "devastating contrivance" that could "wipe out every living being for miles." J. J. Perling wrote an article telling how Napier kept his discovery secret and refused to reveal it, even on his deathbed. Reading the article, Albert Einstein felt compelled to write the author and explain why he had urged President Franklin Roosevelt to develop the atomic bomb, although he wished that it had been possible for the bomb's inventors to die with their discovery unknown, as had John Napier. J. J. Perling released Einstein's comments for publication shortly before the death of the great scientist whose equation $e = mc^2$ laid the basis for atomic power.

Dear Mr. Perling,

The unrevealed invention of Napier interested me very much. I am firmly convinced that Napier did the right thing, not to make his idea public. The same would have been the case with the atomic bomb if those physicists who were working in this field would not have had to fear that the Germans would be the first to produce such a bomb. It is frightful to imagine what a disaster it would have been for the world if Hitler would have come into possession of this weapon, and in such a way would have been able to subjugate humanity and mold it in his image. . . .

A. Einstein

JAPANESE-AMERICANS AFTER PEARL HARBOR

DISPLAY THEIR LOYALTY AND BRAVERY AGAINST THE ENEMY

T he discrimination against Japanese living in California, Oregon, and Washington led to their resentment against Americans. Fearful of an attack upon the West Coast after Pearl Harbor, the U.S. military questioned the loyalty of the Nisei. To avoid possible sabotage and espionage, 120,000 Japanese-Americans were taken from their homes and placed in "relocation centers"—a euphemism for concentration camps—far from the coast.

Uncomplaining, many of the Nisei volunteered for service with the U.S. Army. December 7, 1981, marked the fortieth anniversary of Pearl Harbor. The newspaper columnist Abigail Van Buren asked readers where they were on that "day of infamy." One of the most interesting of 20,000 responses came from a Nisei.

Tucson, Ariz.

I was 19 and living in Yoder, Wyo., when I first heard the news of Pearl Harbor. I canceled my plans to enter the university and enlisted in the Army, where I was to spend the next four years. I served in Italy with the famous 442d regiment, which was made up of Japanese-Americans. It was known as the 'Go for Broke' regiment, the most decorated unit in American history. Daniel Inouye, who later became a senator from Hawaii, was a member of that unit. He lost an arm in battle.

Hashime Saito

FDR's Request to a Future President

TO HONOR AMERICA'S FIRST HERO IN WORLD WAR II

J ust after the United States declared war on Japan on December 8, 1941, America's Captain Colin P. Kelly, Jr., became the first hero to give his life for his country. Besieged on all sides, with Germany and Italy declaring war and Japan swiftly invading American territory in the Pacific, President Franklin Roosevelt still found time to address a letter to the man who would be president in 1956. Roosevelt asked that Captain Kelly's son be given an appointment to West Point "as a token of the nation's appreciation of the heroic services of his father."

The president in 1956, Dwight D. Eisenhower, did not forget. Colin P. Kelly III received his appointment, signed by the commander-in-chief.

December 17, 1941

To the President of the United States in 1956:

I am writing this letter as an act of faith in the destiny of our country. I desire to make a request which I make in full confidence that we shall achieve a glorious victory in the war we are now waging to preserve our democratic way of life.

My request is that you consider the merits of a young American youth of goodly heritage—Colin P. Kelly III, for appointment as a candidate in the United States Military Academy at West Point. I make this appeal in behalf of this youth as a token of the nation's appreciation of the heroic services of his father who met his death in the line of duty at the very outset of the struggle which was thrust upon us by the perfidy of a professed friend.

In the conviction that the service and example of Captain Colin P. Kelly, Jr., will be long remembered, I ask for this consideration in behalf of Colin P. Kelly III.

Franklin D. Roosevelt

GENERAL WAINWRIGHT'S LAST
MESSAGE FROM CORREGIDOR

❧

BEFORE THE INFAMOUS "DEATH MARCH"

*F*ollowing the fall of Manila, General Jonathan Wainwright took *his troops to Bataan and the rock of Corregidor. After holding out for three months against far superior Japanese forces, Wainwright informed President Franklin Roosevelt that it was his duty to surrender "to end this useless effusion of blood."*

After the surrender, the American and Filipino soldiers were taken on the infamous "death march" where thousands more died.

Wainwright was one of the fortunate few to survive three years of imprisonment and torture. Returning a hero, he stood next to General Douglas MacArthur on the U.S.S. Missouri to accept the Japanese surrender ending the war.

1942

Dear Mr. President,

... With many guns and anti-aircraft fire-control equipment destroyed, we are no longer able to prevent accurate bombardment from the air. With numerous batteries of heavy caliber emplaced on the shores of Bataan and Cavite, the enemy now brings devastating crossfire to bear on us, outranging our remaining guns.

Most of my batteries, seacoast, anti-aircraft and field, have been put out of action by the enemy. I have ordered the others destroyed to prevent them from falling into enemy hands. In addition, we are now overwhelmingly assaulted by Japanese troops on Corregidor.

There is a limit to human endurance, and that limit has long since been past. Without prospect of relief, I feel it is my duty to my country and to my gallant troops to end this useless effusion of blood and human sacrifice.

If you agree, Mr. President, please say to the nation that my troops and I have accomplished all that is humanly possible and that we have upheld the best traditions of the United States and its Army.

May God bless and preserve you and guide you and the nation in the effort of ultimate victory.

With profound regret and with continued pride in my gallant troops I go to meet the Japanese commander. Good-by, Mr. President.

Jonathan Wainwright

ANNE MORROW LINDBERGH'S ELOQUENT WELCOME

⌒∽∕∕∕⌒

TO HER FAMOUS HUSBAND RETURNING FROM THE WAR

When Charles A. Lindbergh flew solo across the Atlantic in his single-engine Spirit of St. Louis, on May 21, 1927, he became an instant world-famous hero. Years later, as a member of America First, an organization that opposed the United States' entry into the war against Hitler, his fame turned to infamy. He was accused of being a traitor and a Nazi. Then came Pearl Harbor and Lindbergh proclaimed, "Now [war] has come we must meet it as united Americans regardless of our attitude in the past . . . ," and he offered his services to the air force but was turned down.

Lindbergh resigned his commission as colonel,* yet as a civilian

---

*After the war, Lindbergh served as special consultant to the secretary of the air force. In 1954, Dwight Eisenhower restored his commission at the higher rank of brigadier general.

observer he flew more than fifty combat missions with marine and air force squadrons. Anticipating his return from the Pacific, Anne Morrow Lindbergh, one of the most eloquent letter writers, addressed this welcoming message to her husband.

> July 2, 1944
> Train-Chicago-
> San Francisco

Dear Charles,

I am on my way west. I hope to meet you. I feel madly extravagant and altogether mad, speeding over the country with not much certainty of when or where I'll meet you.

But I feel happy tonight. I have sat and watched the cornfields of Iowa darken, seen the homesteads pass by—a white house, a red barn and a brave cluster of green trees in the midst of oceans of flat fields, like an oasis in a desert. And I have been overcome by the beauty and richness of this country I have flown over so many times with you. And overcome with the beauty and richness of our life together, those early mornings setting out, those evenings gleaming with rivers and lakes below us, still holding the last light. Those fields of daisies we landed on, and dusty fields and desert stretches. Memories of many skies and many earths beneath us—many days, many nights of stars. "How are the waters of the world sweet—if we should die, we have drunk them. If we should sin or separate—if we should fail or secede—we have tasted of happiness—we must be written in the book of the blessed. We have had what life could give. We have eaten of the tree of knowledge, we have known—we have been the mystery of the universe."

> Anne

COMMANDER JOHN KENNEDY

DISPLAYS EXCEPTIONAL COURAGE IN WORLD WAR II

Few acts of courage can match twenty-one-year-old John F. Kennedy's rescue of most of his crew when his PT boat was rammed and sunk by a Japanese destroyer off the island of New Georgia. Thrown into the water, flaming with gasoline, Kennedy towed one man to safety by holding his life jacket with his teeth. He wrote a friend, "They believed us lost for a week—but luckily thank God—they did not send the telegrams—but unfortunately some telegrams will have to be sent." In this letter to his parents, he deplored the loss of so many American fighting men who gave their lives for their country.

[Dear Folks,]

On the bright side of an otherwise completely black time was the way that everyone stood up to it. Previous to that I had become somewhat cynical about the American as a fighting man. I had seen too much bellyaching and laying off. But with the chips down—that all faded away. I can now believe—which I never would have before—the stories of Bataan and Wake. For an American it's got to be awfully easy or awfully tough. When it's in the middle, then there's trouble.

It was a terrible thing though, losing those two men. One had ridden with me for as long as I had been out here. He had been somewhat shocked by a bomb that had landed near the boat about two weeks before. He never really got over it; he always seemed to have the feeling that something was going to happen to him. He never said anything about being put ashore—he didn't want to go—but the next time we came down the line I was going to let him work on the base force. When a fellow gets the feeling that he's in for it, the only thing to do is to let him get off the boat because strangely enough, they always seem to be the ones that do get it. . . . He had a wife and three kids. The other fellow had just come aboard. He was only a kid himself. . . .

When I read that we will fight the Japs for years if necessary and will sacrifice hundreds of thousands if we must—I always like to check from where he is talking—it's seldom out here. People get too used to talking about billions of dollars and millions of soldiers that thousands of dead sounds like a drop in the bucket. But if those thousands want to live as much as the ten I saw— they should measure their words with great, great care.

John

COLONEL McAULIFFE DEFIES THE GERMAN DEMAND

TO SURRENDER THE ENCIRCLED TOWN OF BASTOGNE

Ith a *"last desperate lunge," the German Panzer Divisions surrounded American troops in the Battle of the Bulge. When the situation looked precarious for the U.S. troops, the German commander demanded their surrender. On Christmas Eve, 1944, the U.S. commander, Colonel Anthony Clement McAuliffe, addressed this message to his men, telling of his famous answer to the German commander.*

HEADQUARTERS 101ST AIRBORNE DIVISION
Office of the Division Commander

24 December 1944

MERRY CHRISTMAS

What's Merry about all this, you ask? We're fighting—it's cold—we aren't home. All true but what has the proud Eagle Division accomplished with its worthy comrades of the 10th

Armored Division, the 705th Tank Destroyer Battalion and all the rest? Just this: We have stopped cold everything that has been thrown at us from the North, East, South and West. We have identifications from four German Panzer Divisions, two German Infantry Divisions and one German Parachute Division. These units, spearheading the last desperate German lunge, were headed straight west for key points when the Eagle Division was hurriedly ordered to stem the advance. How effectively this was done will be written in history; not alone in our Division's glorious history but in world history. The Germans actually did surround us—their radios blared our doom. Their Commander demanded our surrender in the following impudent arrogance:

* * *

To the U.S.A. Commander of the encircled town of Bastogne:

The fortune of war is changing. This time the U.S.A. forces in and near Bastogne have been encircled by strong German armored units. More German armored units have crossed the river Ourthe near Ortheuville, have taken Marche and reached St. Hubert by passing through Hombres-Sibret-Tillet. Libramont is in German hands.

There is only one possibility to save the encircled U.S.A. Troops from total annihilation: that is the honorable surrender of the encircled town. In order to think it over a term of two hours will be granted beginning with the presentation of this note.

If this proposal should be rejected one German Artillery Corps and six heavy A.A. Battalions are ready to annihilate the U.S.A. Troops in the near Bastogne. The order for firing will be given immediately after this two hours' term.

All the serious civilian losses caused by this Artillery fire would not correspond with the well known American humanity.

THE GERMAN
COMMANDER

* * *

The German Commander received the following reply:

22 December 1944

To the German Commander:

NUTS!

THE AMERICAN
COMMANDER

* * *

Allied Troops are counterattacking in force. We continue to hold Bastogne. By holding Bastogne we assure the success of the Allied Armies. We know that our Division Commander, General Taylor, will say: "Well Done!"

We are giving our country and our loved ones at home a worthy Christmas present and being privileged to take part in this gallant feat of arms are truly making for ourselves a Merry Christmas.

McAuliffe,
COMMANDING.

HARRY TRUMAN'S FIRST NIGHT IN THE WHITE HOUSE

GERMANY'S SURRENDER: "SOME BIRTHDAY PRESENT"

Franklin D. Roosevelt had died suddenly on April 12, 1945. A stunned Harry Truman found himself president of the United States. The war was still on, but the fighting in Europe was nearing the end. Truman moved into the White House on May 7. The following day, he sent a letter to "Dear Mama & Mary," telling of his first night in the White House and of a wonderful present he was about to receive on his sixty-first birthday. Other presidents' letters may be more eloquent, but none is more human and lively than Harry's personal letters to his folks back home in Independence.

May 8, 1945

Dear Mama & Mary:

I am sixty-one this morning, and I slept in the President's room in the White House last night. They have finished the painting and have some of the furniture in place. I'm hoping it will all be ready for you by Friday. My expensive gold pen doesn't work as well as it should.

This will be a historical day. At 9:00 o'clock this morning I must make a broadcast to the country: announcing the German surrender. The papers were signed yesterday morning and hostilities will cease on all fronts at midnight tonight. Isn't that some birthday present?

Have had one heck of a time with the Prime Minister of Great Britain. He, Stalin and the U.S. President made an agreement to release the news all at once from the three capitals at an hour that would fit us all. We agreed on 9 A.M. Washington time which is 3 P.M. London and 4 P.M. Moscow time.

Mr. Churchill began calling me at daylight to know if we shouldn't make an immediate release without considering the Russians. He was refused and then he kept pushing me to talk to Stalin. He finally had to stick to the agreed plan—but he was mad as a wet hen.

Things have moved at a terrific rate here since April 12. Never a day has gone by that some momentous decision didn't have to be made. So far luck has been with me. I hope it keeps up. It can't stay with me forever however and I hope when the mistake comes it won't be too great to remedy.

We are looking forward to a grand visit with you. I may not be able to come for you as planned but I'm sending the safest, finest plane and all kinds of help so please don't disappoint me.

Lots & lots of love to you both.

Harry

DuPont Receives Its $1

FOR OPERATING THE MANHATTAN PROJECT
IN PASCO

When the atomic bomb was being developed, E. I. DuPont de Nemours & Co. secretly constructed and operated for the government the mammoth Hanford Engineer Works near Pasco, Washington. For this gigantic undertaking the DuPont Company was to receive a fixed fee of $1. In the final accounting, a payment of 68¢ only was allowed, which prompted the president of the Pasco Kiwanis Club to write as follows:

August 11, 1945

Mr. Walter S. Carpenter, Jr., President
E. I. DuPont de Nemours & Co.
Wilmington, Delaware

Dear Mr. Carpenter:

At the last regular meeting of the Pasco Kiwanis Club a resolution was passed which reads as follows:

"An article in a local newspaper states that the DuPont Company received only One Dollar profit from the operations at the Hanford plant and that an expense item of thirty-two cents was not allowed by an accountant, leaving a balance of sixty-eight cents. Thirty-two members of this club are contributing one cent each to make up the difference and also placing their signatures to this letter."

We are proud to be so closely situated to the Hanford project, and all of us feel very sincerely that we have had a part in this magnificent enterprise. We also hope that the Lord will see fit to direct the future efforts and achievements of this product into the right chanel for the good of all mankind.

Sincerely yours,
Mel Swanson, President

Amused by the whimsical gesture and appreciative of the spirit in which it was given, the president of DuPont replied:

E. I. DUPONT DE NEMOURS AND CO.
Wilmington, Delaware

August 30th 1945

Mr. Mel Swanson, President
Pasco Kiwanis Club
Pasco, Washington

Dear Mr. Swanson:

I appreciate sincerely the efforts of you and your associates to restore the solvency of our operation at Hanford. This good-humored gesture of friendliness on your part brings pleasure to all of us. We have always regarded our one dollar fee for the Hanford work as satisfactory compensation.

In fact, so highly do we prize the spirit which led you to write your amusing letter and send us the 32 cents, that we are placing both the letter and the contribution in our company museum for permanent record. It is a most appropriate addition to the various archives and mementoes of sentimental significance of DuPont history.

Please accept our thanks and assurances of appreciation for the cooperation and generosity shown us by the people of the Pasco area. The exacting industrial assignment carried out there, amid conditions calling for utmost discretion from the community, could not have been fulfilled without your able and unstinting assistance. Your forebearance and understanding, under trying circumstances, have been invaluable.

We join fervently in your prayers that the future of atomic energy can be directed toward the benefit and advancement of the human race. We recognize, with you, the national responsibility involved. I am confident, however, that the unity and devotion of the many who had a part in the success of the project will in the end succeed also in turning it to the good of all men.

Yours sincerely,
W. S. Carpenter, Jr.

AN UNSIGNED CHRISTMAS CARD

✍

"I, TOO, HAVE NOT FORGOTTEN"

Every Christmas since 1945, the parents of a young soldier killed at Okinawa had received an unsigned card. It read only, "I, too, have not forgotten." Then, five years later, they received a signed letter explaining the mystery with a most heart-warming denouement.

Dear Folks:

This year I am not sending a card, but an explanation. Perhaps I have been too mysterious, but I was ashamed to sign those cards. You see, your son Carl gave his life to save mine. He was a wonderful guy and had so much to live for, and for five years I have searched for the reason—I knew there must be some purpose I was to fulfill.

Some two months ago I found the answer. I had gone back into the Army a year ago and two months back I received some replacements in my company here. One of them was Carl's kid brother, your youngest boy, Edward. Out of millions that might have been sent, I got Eddie. I feel better, I'll fight better, and let me tell you—I'll take care of that boy. Carl knows it, and I wanted you to know it too.

Respectfully,
Robert Peterson, Capt.

ACE AVIATOR EDDIE RICKENBACKER

WOULD "ELIMINATE THE HATES FROM OUR HEARTS"

An ace aviator in World War I, Eddie Rickenbacker flew special missions for the secretary of war in World War II. On one of his flights, Rickenbacker's plane was forced down in the Pacific. He miraculously survived twenty-four days on a life raft until he was rescued.

After the war, Rickenbacker wrote his friend Harry Vissering, inventor and supporter of the Goodyear blimp, expressing hopes for a new era of mutual respect and understanding for all mankind.

Dear Harry:—

For many years past, including a few years prior to and during World War II, the main objective of our leadership—Government and otherwise, as well as propaganda artists—was to teach the American people—men, women and children—how to hate the Germans and Japs.

This was done through the media of newspapers, radio, moving pictures, billboards, posters, magazine articles and speeches.

On V-E day and finally on V day, the guns were silenced on the battlefields of the world. The dead were buried and the maimed and sick were brought back home—some minus legs, others minus arms, and some even blind.

The hospitals still have untold thousands and, no doubt, will keep some of them until they pass on to another world. Thousands have gone home to their families and been assimilated into the daily peacetime activities.

All of this was a signal for Peace, Love and Good Will toward men, but since the hate was instilled in the hearts and minds of millions, and there were no more Germans and Japs to hate, we started to hate our Allies and to hate ourselves.

Republicans hate Democrats, and Democrats hate Republicans. Communists are being hated. Fascists are being hated. And, last but not least, employees have been taught to hate the boss, the company for which they work, and the stockholders who own it.

Switching the strife from the battlefields of foreign lands to the battlefields on the home front is bringing about disorganization, industrial strife, misery and, if continued, the one and only end—poverty.

Let us then take inventory of ourselves and our pet hates as we approach the Holiday Season, with the hope that we may again recapture our respect and admiration for our fellow men, eliminate the hates from our hearts and minds, and proceed with the teachings of Christ, so that once again we may enjoy the Peace and Tranquillity of the laws and liberties of this great land of ours.

Eddie

NO GUARANTEE OF SECURITY

EVEN WITH BIG ARMS BUILDUP

The advocates of huge buildups in armaments might ponder the words of these three well-known Americans.

James Forrestal, Harry Truman's secretary of defense, tells Hanson Baldwin, military editor of the New York Times, *that there is no such thing as absolute security.*

Lyndon B. Johnson, in a letter to Secretary of State Dean Rusk, concludes through bitter experience that arms can never make us invulnerable to enemies.

Some forty years earlier, Calvin Coolidge stated that he was opposed to any policy of competition in armaments.

Dear Hanson:

It has long been one of my strongly held beliefs that the word "security" ought to be stricken from the language and the word "risk" substituted. The great danger in any country is for people to believe that there is anything absolute about security. Air power, atomic bombs, wealth—by itself none of these give any guaranty. . . .

James F.

Dear Rusk,—

As you know, the establishment and the development of the East-West Center has been a matter of personal interest to me, so I am very happy to have the Commission's report that remarkable progress has been made in the brief period since it was authorized.

I was proud to have had the privilege of presenting the dedication address for the Center in May of 1961. The report quotes from that address a comment which I would re-emphasize today: "Arms can never make us invulnerable nor our enemies invincible, but the support we give to education can make freedom irresistible."

I hope the report can be read widely.

Lyndon B. Johnson

December 3, 1924

Message to Congress:

We have been constantly besought to engage in competitive armaments. Frequent reports will reach us of the magnitude of the military equipment of other nations. We shall do well to be little impressed by such reports or such actions. Any nation undertaking to maintain a military establishment with aggressive and imperialistic designs will find itself severely handicapped in the economic development of the world. I believe thoroughly in the army and navy, in adequate defence and preparation. But I am opposed to any policy of competition in building and maintaining land or sea armaments. . . .

Calvin Coolidge

FOR PEACE AND ALBERT SCHWEITZER

⁄⁊⁊⁊

A YOUNG BLACK'S IDEA BRINGS AID TO HUMANITY

R obert Hill, the thirteen-year-old black son of an American air force sergeant stationed in Naples, had an idea. He sent this letter to the NATO commander in Italy.

Dear General Lindsay:

I have read in the newspapers about people wanting peace. My father has told me about NATO, and that it is also for peace.

I read about Dr. Albert Schweitzer's help to people in Equatorial Africa. . . . This is why I am writing to you. I think that by helping others we can have peace.

I want to help Dr. Schweitzer. I asked my father to buy some medicine and he said he will buy all he can afford if there is a way to get it to Dr. Schweitzer. I thought that if any of your airplanes go where Dr. Schweitzer is, they would deliver it for me. Maybe some other people will want to give some medicine too. . . . I have not told my father I am writing you but I am sure he wouldn't object.

Thank you General if you can help.

Robert A. Hill

General Lindsay promised to send the medicine to Africa. He also arranged to have Bobby's letter broadcast in four languages over the Italian radio network.

Medical supplies valued at $400,000 poured in. With the contributions came letters like this one from Italy, addressed to the thirteen-year-old Negro boy in Waycross, Georgia.

Vomero, Italy

Dear Little Boy:

When I was a child I met a boy of your race in Calabria. Everyone looked at him without speaking and made him unhappy. One day I went to him and started to talk. Together we understood the sea, the sky, the beauty of things. And he was no longer unhappy. . . . You represent the soul of all the children in the world. Bring my love with you to America.

Signora——

Bobby Hill was flown with the supplies to Lambarene, Africa. When he left, Dr. Schweitzer gave him a rosewood box—for his mother—containing this note:

Dear Mrs. Hill:

Any mother who can bear a child like yours deserves my highest esteem.

Albert Schweitzer

LYNDON B. JOHNSON'S ANSWER TO RACISM

HE REGRETS THAT PREJUDICE EXTENDS EVEN BEYOND LIFE

rivate Felix Longoria was killed in action in the Philippines near the end of World War II. Three and a half years later his young widow arranged to have his body sent to his home town of Three Rivers, Texas, for reburial. But the only undertaker in the town refused to perform the services, saying that "other white people objected to the use of the funeral home by people of Mexican origin." When the president of a veteran's organization complained, Lyndon B. Johnson, then a senator, replied:

Washington
January 12, 1949

Dr. Hector P. Garcia, President
American G.I. Forum
Corpus Christi, Texas

Dear Sir,

I deeply regret to learn that the prejudice of some individuals extends even beyond this life.

I have no authority over civilian funeral homes, nor does the Federal Government. However, I have today made arrangements to have Felix Longoria reburied with full military honors in Arlington National Cemetery here at Washington where the honored dead of our nation's wars rest. . . .

Lyndon B. Johnson

A LOYAL FIRST-FAMILY AMERICAN

GOES BACK ON THE WARPATH

A Cherokee Indian mother who had lost two boys in World War II wrote General Clifton B. Cates, Commandant of the Marine Corps, appealing to have her last surviving son transferred from the fighting front in Korea to a noncombat zone. The sympathizing general complied.

From his new assignment, a desk job in Tokyo, young Robert J. Ward explained to his mother why he felt compelled to go back "on the warpath."

Dec. 1, 1950

Dear Mother:

I'm no hero, but I also have responsibilities to little squaw [his daughter] and Bettye [his wife] and you.

If these people aren't stopped here on their own ground, we will have to share the thing so many have died to prevent their loved ones from sharing, the sight of death in our own backyard; of women and children being victims of these people.

I went on the warpath for the right to do my bit to keep our people free and proud and now I'm shackled to a useless job.

I ask you, my mother, to free me so I can once again be free to help my boys.

They placed their faith in me and I brought them all back and now someone else leads them and I know they need me.

Maybe in a sense I need them, my dirty, stinking and loyal platoon.

Once I cried before you when I thought I'd lost someone whom I loved very dearly, and once again did I cry when I was told I must leave my men.

So I ask you the one thing which your heart does not want to do, release me to fight.

I pace my room feeling useless, being no good to anyone. I'm no barracks, parade-ground marine. I'm a Cherokee Indian and I'm happiest being miserable with my own people up on those mountains.

I know you'll understand that your blessings will go with me into whatever the future holds in store for us.

Write to the commandant and release me, explain to them as only you can that I have a job to do and that you understand.

Your loving son,
Robert

On December 16, the courageous mother of one of America's first families wrote the letter requested.

"WE'RE LOSING THE RACE BY INCHES"

❧

EMPHATICALLY WARNED DR. EDWARD TELLER

One reason that America had been lagging behind in the science race was our failure to convert to the metric system. That was the opinion of Dr. Edward Teller, "father of the hydrogen bomb," as expressed to San Francisco newsman Allen Brown twenty years ago.

More recently, American scientists have been switching to metrics, but Mr. and Mrs. Average Citizen are still having trouble buying gasoline by the liter and figuring distances by the kilometer.

Dear Mr. Brown:

This is a subject on which I am rabid.

In 1927, the Russians did away with whatever versts and other absurd units they were using and, like most of the rest of the world, they completely adopted the metric system. Also relatively recently, the Hindus and the Japanese have adopted it. But there are still some wild Anglo-Saxon tribes which cherish their traditions above everything else. Let me mention a few of these traditions:

It is said that King Henry I established the yard by measuring the distance between the tip of his finger and the tip of his nose.

An inch is three, dry, round barleycorns laid end to end, according to the pronouncement of King Edward II.

The mile comes from the Latin "mille" or thousand, and was determined by the thousand double steps of the average Roman soldier.

Before improving their ways with the metric system, the French once had a unit of measure called the "journal." The journal was the area a farmer could cultivate in one day with his plow.

In Noah's time carpenters had a measurement called the cubit.

This was the length of the forearm from the tip of the middle finger to the elbow. Assuming that several carpenters with several different arm-lengths worked on the same project, it is a wonder that the ark floated.

And there is a story that the erudite German, Gabriel Daniel Fahrenheit, once waited in Danzig until it had got as cold as he thought it could possibly get. Then, on the very cold day, he stuck his thermometer out the window, and that became <u>zero</u>. Then he put it under his arm. That became <u>100 degrees</u>. So the history of our system of temperature supposedly goes back to the fact that there was once, in a rather cold town, a rather hot guy!

Edward Teller

EISENHOWER DEFENDS THE PICTURE ON HIS WALL

ACCLAIMS ROBERT E. LEE AS A GREAT AMERICAN

When Dwight D. Eisenhower occupied the White House, he proudly displayed pictures of Washington, Franklin, Lincoln, and Robert E. Lee in his Oval Office.

After calling them all great Americans in one of his speeches, Ike received a letter from an indignant citizen: "How can you honor Lee, a man who sought to destroy the country you lead?"

Eisenhower's reply dispelled all doubts as to Lee's patriotic qualities.

Washington, D.C.
August 18, 1960

Dear Dr. Scott:

Gen. Robert E. Lee was, in my estimation, one of the supremely gifted men produced by our nation. He believed unswervingly in the constitutional validity of his cause, which until

1865 was still an arguable question in America; he was a poised and inspiring leader, true to the high trust reposed in him by millions of his fellow citizens. . . .

From deep conviction I simply say this: A nation of men of Lee's calibre would be unconquerable in spirit and soul. Indeed, to the degree that present-day American youth will strive to emulate his painstaking efforts to help heal the nation's wounds once the bitter struggle was over, we, in our own time of danger in a divided world, will be strengthened and our love of freedom sustained.

Such are the reasons I proudly display the picture of the great American on my office wall.

Dwight D. Eisenhower

MRS. JOHN D. ROCKEFELLER II
BESEECHES HER SONS

TO SHUN RACE PREJUDICES AND HATRED

W hen three of her sons were attending college, Mrs. John D. Rockefeller II wrote to them of "one of the greatest causes of evil in the world." Throughout his life, Nelson Rockefeller always endeavored to live up to his mother's standards and in most cases succeeded.

Dear John, Nelson and Laurance,

For a long time I had very much on my mind, and heart, a certain subject. I meant to bring it up at prayers, and then later have it for a question to be discussed at a family council. But the right time, because of your father's illness, never seemed to come.

Out of my experience and observations, has grown the earnest conviction that one of the greatest causes of evil in the world is race hatred and race prejudice. In other words, the feeling of dislike that a person or nation has against another person or nation, without just cause, an unreasoning aversion is another way to express it.

The two peoples or races who suffer most from this treatment are the Jews and the Negroes. But some people "hate" the Italians, who in turn hate the Yugoslavs, who hate the Austrians, who hate the Czechoslovaks, and so it goes endlessly.

You boys are still young. No group of people has ever done you a personal injury. You have no inherent dislikes. I want to make an appeal to your sense of fair play, and to beseech you to begin your lives as young men by giving the other fellow . . . a fair chance and a square deal. . . .

Put yourselves in the place of an honest, poor man who happens to belong to one of the so-called "despised" races. Think of having no friendly hand held out to you. No kindly look. No pleasant, encouraging word spoken to you. What I would like you always to do is what I try humbly to do myself. That is, never to say or do anything that would wound the feelings or the self respect of any human being. And to give special consideration to all who are in any way repressed.

That is what your father does naturally, from the firmness of his nature, and the kindness of his heart. I long to have our family stand firmly for what is best and highest in life. It isn't always easy. But it is worthwhile.

Your Mother

THE MOONS OF SATURN
◦◦◦◦◦◦
HOW MANY ARE THERE?

When William Beebe was teaching astronomy at Yale, he flunked Elbert Hamlin for giving too many moons* to Saturn. Fifteen years later, Hamlin, then a distinguished

*More recently, Voyager I and II's spectacular probes of Saturn revealed fifteen or more moons around Saturn. So Judge Hamlin was incorrect not for giving too many satellites but for giving too few!

judge, learned of the discovery of a few additional moons and sent this letter to Professor Beebe.

Professor William Beebe
Yale University
New Haven, Conn.

Dear Professor,

Fifteen years ago you flunked me not knowing that my knowledge of Saturn exceeded yours. And your flunking me was a tragedy for Yale. There was the golden opportunity which would have given Yale University immortality in science by announcing a discovery fifteen years ahead of all other institutions of learning. I can forgive you for the personal insult, but it is difficult to forgive you when we remember what my discovery would have meant in adding prestige to Yale.

Elbert Hamlin

THE FATAL PRESIDENTIAL CYCLE SINCE 1840

IN YEARS ENDING IN ZERO, NO PRESIDENT LIVED OUT HIS TERM

After the election in 1960, a California writer reminded John F. Kennedy of the ominous coincidence that since 1840 no U.S. president elected in a year ending in a zero (every twenty years) had lived out his term. William Henry Harrison, 1840, died of pneumonia only one month after his inauguration; Warren G. Harding, 1920, succumbed to a fatal ailment. Franklin Roosevelt (1940) died of a stroke. Lincoln (1860), Garfield (1880), McKinley (1900), and Kennedy (1960) were all assassinated. Not knowing his *fate, JFK responded to the California Cassandra with his usual sense of humor. Ronald Reagan, elected in 1980, fortunately survived the bullets of an attempted assassination.*

Dear Mr. Squires:

I feel that the future will have to answer this for itself—both as to my aspirations and my fate should I have the privilege of occupying the White House. I dare say, should anyone take this phenomenon to heart, anyone, that is, who aspires to change his address to 1600 Pennsylvania Avenue, that most probably the landlord would be left from 1960–64 with a "For Rent" sign hanging on the gatehouse door.

Sincerely,
John F. Kennedy

LEE HARVEY OSWALD SWEARS REVENGE

BEFORE ASSASSINATING PRESIDENT KENNEDY

T he twenty-year omen came true when President John F. Kennedy was assassinated after his "thousand days" in office by Lee Harvey Oswald in Dallas. Many investigations failed to prove that the fatal shooting was part of a conspiracy. This letter written to John B. Connally, ten days after Kennedy's inauguration, seems to support the investigators' findings. However, it has been revealed that one month before he shot President Kennedy, Oswald traveled to Mexico, where he met at the Soviet embassy with an officer of the KGB Thirteenth Department, which controls sabotage and assassinations.

Lee H. Oswald
U.S.M.C.R. 1653250
Valinina St. 4-29
Minsk, U.S.S.R.
January 30, 1961

Secretary of the Navy
John B. Connally Jr.
Fort Worth, Texas

Dear Sir:

I wish to call your attention to a case about which you may have personal knowledge since you are a resident of Ft. Worth as I am.

In November 1958 an event was well publicated in the Ft. Worth newspapers concerning a person who had gone to the Soviet Union to reside for a short time (much in the same way E. Hemingway resided in Paris.)

This person in answer to questions put to him by reporters in Moscow criticized certain facets of American life. The story was turned into another "turncoat" sensation with the result that the Navy Department gave this person a belated dishonourable discharge although he had received an honorable discharge after three years service on Sept. 11, 1957 at El Toro, Marine Corps base in California.

These are the basic facts of *my* case.

I have and always had the full sanction of the U.S. Embassy, Moscow, U.S.S.R. and hence the U.S. government. In as much as I am returning to the U.S.A. in this year with the aid of the U.S. Embassy, bring with me my family (since I married in the U.S.S.R.) I shall employ all means to right this gross mistake or injustice to a boni-fied U.S. citizen and ex-service man. The U.S. government has no charges or complaints against me. I ask you to look into this case and take the necessary steps to repair the damage done to me and my family. For information I would direct you to consult the American Embassy, Chikovski St. 19121, Moscow, U.S.S.R.

Thank you,
Lee H. Oswald

ST. PETER'S CHURCH DUNS THE BRITISH

∽∽∽

FOR A FENCE DAMAGED DURING THE REVOLUTION

I n 1961 the Rector of St. Peter's Church of Philadelphia, with a keen eye for humor and the exponential growth of compound interest, dunned the British Exchequer for the cost of the church's fence, torn down for firewood by the Redcoats in Revolutionary days. Estimating the cost to be $18, he thought it only fair that he be paid 6 percent interest, compounded annually for the 183 years since the damage was done. At that rate, the interest would total $769,565.96. With equal good humor and witty reasoning, Chancellor Lloyd suggested a solution based on St. Paul's Epistle to the Corinthians.

August 11th, 1961

The Rt. Hon. Selwyn Lloyd, CBE, TD, QC, MP
Chancellor of Exchequer
Whitehall, London, S.W.1

Sir,

St. Peter's Church will celebrate its bicentennial on September 10, and we are desirous of starting our Third Century of Worship after that date with all accounts settled. Therefore, we must ask you to reimburse this Parish for a quantity of firewood obtained by British Troops in the Winter of 1777–78 by the expedient of tearing down our fence.

Mr. Frank E. Seymour, our Accounting Warden, has informed me that on February 1, 1778, one Major Edward Williams of the Royal Artillery, wrote to the Reverend Mr. Coombe, then Rector of St. Peter's, stating that his commander, Gen. Pattison, would see that "a reasonable allowance" was made for the fence.

Although a copy of that pledge is included in the Minutes of the Vestry for February, 1778, no such reasonable allowance has been forthcoming.

In view of the length of the fence, which was seasoned at the time, although relatively new, I should judge that a reasonable allowance in 1778 would have been approximately $18.00. There is no legal justification for making any greater demand.

At the same time, it is suggested that 183 years is an unconscionably long time for an indebtedness of this nature to remain unpaid. As a consequence, we in turn would consider it reasonable to ask for the payment of interest at the rate of 6 per centum, compounded annually, in addition to the principal sum of $18.00.

Very truly,
Joseph Koci, Jr.
Rector

The exchequer's reply:

TREASURY CHAMBERS
Great George Street
London, S.W.1.

September 8, 1961

Dear Sir:

The Chancellor of the Exchequer has asked me to thank you for your letter of 11th August, about damage, allegedly done to the fence round your church by British Troops in the winter of 1777–78.

The Chancellor observes that, as this is said to have occurred before the Treaty of Versailles in 1783, Pennsylvania was at that time, a British Colonial territory. The convention is that claims by citizens of Colonial territories against the Government which have not been settled by the date of independence, lie against the successor Government unless a special arrangement is made to the contrary. No such special arrangement can be traced, and, therefore, I am asked to advise that you should refer your claim either to the Federal Government of the U.S.A., or to the State Government of Pennsylvania, as you feel appropriate. . . .

I am however asked by the Chancellor being, as presumably

Major Williams was, of Welsh origin himself and being also formerly an officer in the Royal Artillery, to forward to you his personal cheque for £6.8s. ld. the present equivalent, at $2.81 to the £, of $18, by the way of a contribution to the funds of your Church, and as a token of his deep regard for the American people, in the hope, however, that it will not be considered to prejudice your claim against the Federal Government of the U.S.A., or the State Government of Pennsylvania.

Finally the Chancellor wishes me to convey his very best wishes for your bi-centenary, and to commend to you the words of the fifteenth verse of the third chapter of St. Paul's Epistle to the Corinthians.*

Yours faithfully,
C. J. Carey
Private Secretary

*"If any man's work shall be burned, he shall suffer loss: but he himself shall be saved; yet so as by fire" (I Cor. 3:15).

157 YEARS TOO LATE
UNION COLLEGE ACKNOWLEDGES AN OFFER OF NOAH WEBSTER

I n 1805, Noah Webster wrote to Union College in Schenectady, New York, offering to share the royalties on his newly published Spelling Book. More than a century and a half later, shocked to discover that Webster's letter had never been acknowledged, Union professor Codman Hislop hastened to compose an answer. Less well known than his famous Dictionary, Webster's Spelling Book is reputed to have sold more than 100 million copies, breaking all existing records for best-sellers.

Noah Webster, Jr. <u>Esquire</u>
New Haven, Connecticut

Dear Mr. Webster:

Your letter of June 18, 1805, addressed to the trustees of Union College, has been received and its contents noted. Frankly, in view of your extraordinary offer to the college of that date, their failure to reply was not only rude, it was a dereliction of duty, a betrayal of their trust, and, plainly speaking, poor business.

Poor business did I say? Good Heavens! Considering the fact that in 1805 we had an empty treasury, practically no credit, and a future based on the success of a lottery, the tickets for which had not even been printed, I'd say our failure to acknowledge your offer to endow Union College was, well, a veritable block-buster of a mistake.

I suspect "blockbuster," by the by, as a word is not in that little dictionary you published in 1807; but, then, there were things rooting in the labyrinths of the human mind you couldn't know about, and, of course, there were things we couldn't know about; for instance, how could we know that the little spelling book you mentioned to our trustees back in 1805 was going to sell over one hundred million copies?

This <u>was</u> your offer, wasn't it? ". . . because of my love of literature and learning . . ." (your very words), you said you were ready to give to Union College fifty cents on every thousand copies of that speller printed in New York State. . . . But, as I've already said, Sir, how were we to know that that grandiloquently-titled textbook was to become the famous "blueback speller," a book which throughout all of the nineteenth century was to be outsold only by the Bible? . . .

Well, Mr. Webster, I suspect the fault, and I use that word only because I am wise in my hindsight, the fault was our new president's. . . .

President Nott, Sir, was too full of big schemes to be a tidy, methodical man. . . . Either that, or, in the confusion of the time, he turned it over, let's say, to Tutor Davis, new that year, to answer, and Tutor Davis simply forgot to do it, being frightened out of his wits most of the time by a clique of students who bedeviled him by throwing rocks through his study window. . . .

In any event, Sir, and with much respect, I offer you our belated apologies. We could have used that blueback speller income . . . a hundred million copies sold!

Sincerely yours,
Codman Hislop

THE UNITED STATES NAVY

~~~

GIVES A SPECIAL CHRISTMAS GIFT TO FRANCE
</div>

W*illiam Lederer, coauthor with Eugene Burdick of* The Ugly American, *tells a Christmas Eve story of a different kind of Yankee emissary in this letter to the chief of U.S. Naval* Operations. *If there were more such Americans overseas, the signs* "Yankee Go Home" *would come down throughout the world.*

Admiral David L. McDonald, USN
Chief of Naval Operations
Washington 25, D.C.

<div align="right">
[December 1962]
</div>

Dear Admiral McDonald:

Eighteen people asked me to write this letter to you.

Last year at Christmas time my wife, three boys and I were in France, on our way from Paris to Nice. For five wretched days everything had gone wrong. Our hotels were "tourist traps," our rented car broke down; we were all restless and irritable in the crowded car. On Christmas Eve, when we checked into our hotel in Nice, there was no Christmas spirit in our hearts.

It was raining and cold when we went out to eat. We found a drab little restaurant shoddily decorated for the holiday. Only five tables were occupied. There were two German couples, two French families, and an American sailor, by himself. In the corner a piano player listlessly played Christmas music.

I was too tired and miserable to leave. I noticed that the other customers were eating in stony silence. The only person who seemed happy was the American sailor. While eating, he was writing a letter, and a half-smile lighted his face.

My wife ordered our meal in French. The waiter brought us the wrong thing. I scolded my wife for being stupid. The boys defended her, and I felt even worse.

Then, at the table with the French family on our left, the father slapped one of his children for some minor infraction, and the boy began to cry.

On our right, the German wife began berating her husband.

All of us were interrupted by an unpleasant blast of cold air. Through the front door came an old flower woman. She wore a dripping, tattered overcoat, and shuffled in on wet, rundown shoes. She went from one table to the other.

"Flowers, monsieur? Only one franc."

No one bought any.

Wearily she sat down at a table between the sailor and us. To the waiter she said, "A bowl of soup. I haven't sold a flower all afternoon." To the piano player she said hoarsely, "Can you imagine, Joseph, soup on Christmas Eve?"

He pointed to his empty "tipping plate."

The young sailor finished his meal and got up to leave. Putting on his coat, he walked over to the flower woman's table.

"Happy Christmas," he said, smiling and picking out two corsages. "How much are they?"

"Two francs, Monsieur."

Pressing one of the small corsages flat, he put it into the letter he had written, then handed the woman a 20-franc note.

"I don't have change, Monsieur," she said. "I'll get some from the waiter."

"No, ma'am," said the sailor, leaning over and kissing the ancient cheek. "This is my Christmas present to you."

Then he came to our table, holding the other corsage in front of him. "Sir," he said to me, "may I have permission to present these flowers to your beautiful daughter?"

In one quick motion he gave my wife the corsage, wished us a Merry Christmas and departed.

Everyone had stopped eating. Everyone had been watching the sailor. Everyone was silent.

A few seconds later Christmas exploded throughout the restaurant like a bomb.

The old flower woman jumped up, waving the 20-franc note, shouted to the piano player, "Joseph, my Christmas present! And you shall have half so you can have a feast too."

The piano player began to belt out Good King Wenceslaus, beating the keys with magic hands.

My wife waved her corsage in time to the music. She appeared 20 years younger. She began to sing, and our three sons joined her, bellowing with enthusiasm.

"Gut! Gut!" shouted the Germans. They began singing in German.

The waiter embraced the flower woman. Waving their arms, they sang in French.

The Frenchman who had slapped the boy beat rhythm with his fork against a bottle. The lad climbed on his lap, singing in a youthful soprano.

A few hours earlier 18 persons had been spending a miserable evening. It ended up being the happiest, the very best Christmas Eve, they had ever experienced.

This, Admiral McDonald, is what I am writing you about. As the top man in the Navy, you should know about the very special gift that the U.S. Navy gave to my family, to me and to the other people in that French restaurant. Because your young sailor had Christmas spirit in his soul, he released the love and joy that had been smothered within us by anger and disappointment. He gave us Christmas.

Thank you, Sir, very much.

Merry Christmas,
Bill Lederer

WHY GERALD R. FORD PARDONED RICHARD M. NIXON

⚭

HE JUSTIFIES HIS ACTION TO HIS CRITICS

A*fter Watergate, when impeachment and criminal proceedings seemed inevitable, Gerald R. Ford's pardon of Richard M. Nixon raised a storm of protest and an avalanche of critical mail. Ford adeptly answered his critics by outlining the reasons for his action and summed them up as a concern "to heal the wounds to the Nation."*

THE WHITE HOUSE
WASHINGTON

October, 1974

THANK YOU . . .

While the heavy volume of mail on the pardon of former President Nixon does not allow me to respond personally as I would like, I do want to take this means to let you know how much I appreciate receiving your views on this.

This was not an easy decision to reach, as I am sure you are aware. Before making it, I undertook a thorough examination of the entire matter. This included my right to grant pardons under the Constitution, the legal actions contemplated by the Special Prosecutor, the probable duration of the criminal proceedings and a number of other factors. Throughout this evaluation process, my main concern was to heal the wounds to the Nation. That was the top priority. I know there are deep and genuine differences among good people over the decision I made. But I felt then, and I feel now, that I made the right decision in an honest, conscientious effort to end the divisions in this country. . . .

Sincerely,
Gerald R. Ford

MESSAGE INTO THE COSMOS

❦

FROM PRESIDENT JIMMY CARTER

T*he Voyager spacecraft rocketed into space on its long journey to Jupiter, Saturn, Uranus, and then headed out beyond our solar system for perhaps billions of years. It carried a long-playing recording of earth sounds, including greetings in sixty languages, music, and noises of animals, volcanoes, avalanches, etc.*

Also aboard was a letter to living organisms unknown from President Jimmy Carter containing a declaration, more hopeful than factual, that planet Earth is "rapidly becoming a single global civilization."

This Voyager spacecraft was constructed by the United States of America. We are a community of 240 million human beings among the more than 4 billion who inhabit the planet Earth. We human beings are still divided into nation states, but these states are rapidly becoming a single global civilization.

We cast this message into the cosmos. It is likely to survive a billion years into our future, when our civilization is profoundly altered and the surface of the Earth may be vastly changed.

Of the 200 billion stars in the Milky Way galaxy some— perhaps many—may have inhabited planets and spacefaring civilizations. If one such civilization intercepts Voyager and can understand these recorded contents, here is our message:

This is a present from a small distant world, a token of our sounds, our science, our images, our music, our thoughts and our feelings. We are attempting to survive our time so we may live into yours.

We hope someday, having solved the problems we face, to join a community of galactic civilizations. This record represents our hope and our determination, and our good will in a vast and awesome universe.

Jimmy Carter
President
United States of America

INDEX